WASTE WATER TREATMENT

USING NANOMATERIALS

MUHAMMAD MUNIR

IN THE NAME OF ALLAH WHO IS MOST BENEFICIAL AND MERCIFUL

Dedicated
TO
My loving Parents, Brother, Sister
Who are the Great Asset of my Life
And
My Father
(May his souls rest in peace, Aamin)
Whose Absence is always Felt

TABLE OF CONTENTS

List of abbreviations	iii
List of symbols	v
List of Figures	vi
List of Tables	xv
List of publication	xvi
Abstract	xvii
CHAPTER 1: INTRODUCTION	**1-11**
1.1 Background and Motivation	1
1.2 Nanotechnology	2
1.2.1 Background	3
1.2.2 Why work on the Nanoscale	3
1.2.3 Nanomaterials	4
1.3 Hydrothermal Crystal Growth Technology	7
1.3.1 Background	7
1.3.2 Reactors for Hydrothermal Synthesis	7
1.4 Vanadium	8
1.4.1 Ammonium Metavanadate, NH_4VO_3	10
1.5 Statement of the problem	10
1.6 The objective of the study	11
CHAPTER 2: REVIEW OF LITERATURE	**12-41**
2.1 Nanostructures	12
2.1.1 Types of nanostructures	12
2.1.2 Synthesis of nanostructures	13
2.2 Synthesis of vanadium nanostructures	14
2.3 Characterization of nanostructures	15
2.4 Applications of nanostructures in environmental remediation	16
2.4.1 Removal of contaminants by adsorption	16
2.4.2 Redox catalytic degradation of pollutants	17
2.5 Photocatalytic degradation of contaminants	17

2.5.1 Basic principle of photocatalytic oxidation process		18
2.6 Photocatalytic property of bismuth vanadate nanostractures		20
2.6.1 Microemulsion (MEs) method		22
2.6.2 Flame spray synthesis method		24
2.6.3 Ultrasonic-assisted method		26
2.6.4 Microwave method		27
2.6.5 Coprecipitation method		28
2.6.6 Sol-gel method		29
2.6.7 Hydrothermal method		30
2.6.7.1 Hydrothermal method without any additives		31
2.6.7.2 Hydrothermal method using surfactants		32
2.6.7.3 Hydrothermal method using other additives		33
2.6.8 Modification of $BiVO_4$ with Novel-metal and Non-metal element		33
2.6.8.1 Noble metal deposition		34
2.6.8.2 Metal doping		35
2.6.8.3 Non-metal doping		34
2.7 Preparation of film		36
2.8 Other synthesis method		37
2.9 Zincvanadate nanostructures		39
2.10 Ferricvanadatenanostractures		40
CHAPTER 3: MATERIALS AND METHODS		**42-53**
3.1.	Hydrothermal method	43
3.2.	Photocatalysis	45
3.3	Electrochemical sensing	46
3.4	Experimental setup and working	47
	3.4.1. Synthesis of $BiVO_4$ nanostructures	47
	3.4.2. Synthesis of $FeVO_4$ nanostructures	48
	3.4.3. Synthesis of $Zn_3(VO_4)_2$ nanostructures	49
	3.4.4. Synthesis of $BiVO_4/FeVO_4$ composite	50
	3.4.5. Synthesis of $Zn_3(VO_4)_2/BiVO_4$ composite	52

3.5 Structural Characterization Techniques of MVO nanocomposites   52

CHAPTER 4: RESULTS AND DISCUSSIONS   54-125

4.1 Fabrication of m-BiVO$_4$ Nanoparticles for Photocatalytic Degradation of dyes   54
    4.1.1 Introduction   54
    4.1.2 X-rays diffraction (XRD)   55
    4.1.3 Scanning electron Microscopic (SEM) analysis   56
    4.1.4 Fourier Infrared Spectroscopy (FTIR)   57
    4.1.5 Brunauer-Emmett-Teller (BET) surface area analysis   58
    4.1.6 Photocatalytic activity   59
    4.1.7 Photoluminescence (PL) analysis   62

4.2 Enhanced photocatalytic performance of FeVO$_4$ for dye and waste effluent   65
    4.2.1 Introduction   65
    4.2.2 Scanning Electron Microscopic (SEM) analysis   66
    4.2.2 Energy Dispersive Spectroscopy (EDX)   67
    4.2.3 X-Rays Diffraction (XRD)   68
    4.2.4 Fourier Infrared Spectroscopy (FTIR)   68
    4.2.5 Photocatalytic activity   69
    4.2.6 Brunauer-Emmett-Teller (BET) surface area analysis   74
    4.2.7 Photoluminescence (PL)   74
    4.2.8 Effect of Dose, stability and recyclability   75

4.3 Facile Synthesis of Zinc Vanadate Zn$_3$(VO$_4$)$_2$ for Photocatalytic activity   79
    4.3.1 Introduction   79
    4.3.2 Scanning Electron Microscopy (SEM)   80
    4.3.3 Energy Dispersive Spectroscopy (EDX)   80
    4.3.4 X-Rays Diffraction (XRD)   81
    4.3.5 X-ray photoelectron spectroscopy (XPS)   81
    4.3.6 Fourier Infrared spectroscopy (FTIR)   82
    4.3.7 Photocatalytic activity   83
    4.3.8 Photoluminescence (PL)   89

4.4 photocatalytic degradation of CV dye and detection of A.A using $BiVO_4/FeVO_4$ heterojunction composite 91

    4.4.1 Introduction 91

    4.4.2 X-Rays Diffraction (XRD) and Energy Dispersive Spectroscopy (EDX) 91

    4.3.5 Scanning Electron Microscopy (SEM) 92

    4.4.3 X-ray photoelectron spectroscopy (XPS) 93

    4.4.4 Brunauer–Emmett–Teller (BET) Surface area 95

    4.4.5 Fourier Infrared Spectroscopy (FTIR) 96

    4.4.6 Raman Analysis 97

    4.4.7 Photocatalytic activity 97

    4.4.8 Photoluminescence (PL) 104

    4.4.9 Electrochemical Impedance spectroscopy (EIS) 105

4.5 Synthesis of $Zn_3(VO_4)_2/BiVO_4$ for the photocatalytic degradation of MB dye and electrochemical detection of H_2O_2 109

    4.5.1 Introduction 109

    4.5.2 X-Rays Diffraction (XRD) 109

    4.5.3 Scanning Electron Microscopy (SEM) 110

    4.5.4 Photocatalysis 111

    4.5.5 Photoluminescnce (PL) 117

    4.5.6 Electrochemical Impedance Spectroscopy (EIS) 120

CHAPTER 5: SUMMARY   125-126

1.5 Conclusion and future Recommendations

REFERENCES   127-143

LIST OF ABBREVIATIONS

mm	Millimetre (10^{-3} m)
Mm	Micro meter (10^{-6} m)
Nm	Nanometer (10^{-9} m)
BF	Bright field
DF	Dark field
CBD	Chemical bath deposition
CBED	Convergent Beam Electron Diffraction
GCE	Glassy carbon electrode
eV	Electron volt
FWHM	Full width of half maximum
h	Hours
keV	Kilo electron volt
min	Minutes
PVD	Physical vapour deposition
S	Seconds
SAED	selected area electron diffraction
SEM	Scanning electron microscopy
EDX	Energy dispersive X-ray spectroscopy
TEM	Transmission electron microscopy
XPS	X-ray photoelectron spectroscopy
XRD	X-ray diffraction
FTIR	Fourier transforms infrared
DRS	Diffuse reflectance Spectroscopy
EPR	Electron paramagnetic resonance
BET	Brunauer Emmett Teller
EIS	Electrochemical Impedance Spectroscopy
PL	Photo luminance
CV	Crystal violet
RhB	Rhodamine-B

CR	Congo red
MB	Methylene Blue
MO	Methyl Orange
CTAB	Acetyl trims ethyl ammonium bromide
LED	Light emitting diode
PCD	Photocatalysis decay
AOP	Advance oxidation Process
ESI	Elementary supporting information
Ehp	Electron-hole pair
MVO	Metal vanadate

LIST OF SYMBOLS

Å	Angstrom
a, b, c	Cell parameters
c	speed of light or Concentration of absorbing material or
d	Distance of lattice plane or thickness of absorbing material
E	Energy
Eg	Band gap energy
h	Planck constant
J	emission current density
I	Intensity of transmitted light
I_o	Intensity of incoming light
K	Shape factor
n	Amount of molecule or order of diffraction
p	Pressure
R	gas constant
T	Temperature
U	Voltage or inner energy
V	Volume
v	Frequency
β	Line broadening at the half-maximum intensity
θ	Bragg angle
λ	Wavelength
τ	Domain size or Particle size
V	Vanadium
φ	work function

LIST OF FIGURES

Figure 1.1	(a) and (b) Illustration the increase in surface area to volume ratio.	5
Figure 1.2	(a) A schematic diagram illustrating the changes in electronic density of states that occur as dimensionality is varied from 3D to 0D, assuming free electrons. (b) Quantum confinement is mature for the intensification of energy difference between energy states and band gap.	6
Figure 1.3	Schematic drawing of Experimental autoclave apparatus for hydrothermal crystal growth.	8
Figure 1.4	Reviews the number of papers (percentage of the total amount of papers) of numerous transition metals in the area of material catalysis, which is able to be retrieved in the open literature. The fact that the highest number of papers is published on the vanadium-based catalysts underlines the importance of vanadium in supported metal oxide catalysis.	10
Figure 2.1	Schematic presentation of photocatalytic processes.	11
Figure 2.2	Schematic diagrams illustrating the principle of photocatalysis.	12
Figure 2.3	Number of scientific papers published on $BiVO_4$ based as photocatalyst from the last six years	21
Figure 2.4	Schematic illustration of microemulsion method for the preparation of nanostructure	22
Figure 2.5	The XRD spectrum of microemulsion prepared powder at different temperature (a) 400 °C for 10 min, (b) 400, (c) 500, (d) 600 and (e) 700 °C for 20 min and the solid-state derived $BiVO4$ powders heated at (f) 700 °C for 5 h.	23
Figure 2.6	SEM images of $BiVO4$ nanoparticles prepared at (a) 400, (b) 500, (c) 600 and (d) 700 °C for 20 min $BiVO_4$ powders and (f) solid-state derived $BiVO4$ at 700 °C for 5 h prepared by SSR.	24
Figure 2.7	Schematic diagram of Flame spray method for the preparation of	25

	micro/nanostructure of BiVO$_4$ photocatalyst.	
Figure 2.8	Schematic diagram of ultrasonic-assisted method for the preparation of BiVO$_4$ based product nanostructures.	26
Figure 2.9	Schematic process of microwave-assisted method for the preparation of BiVO$_4$ micro/nanostructures.	27
Figure 2.10	Schematic representation of co-precipitation method for the preparation BiVO$_4$ based nanostructures.	29
Figure 2.11	Schematic illustration of sol-gel method for the preparation of BiVO$_4$ nanostructures.	30
Figure 2.12	Schematic illustrations for the synthesis of BiVO$_4$ via hydrothermal method.	31
Figure 2.13	Schematic diagram of silica template assisted method.	39
Figure 2.14	Schematic diagram for the preparation of BiVO$_4$ nanoproduct by solvothermal method.	43
Figure 3.1	Schematic flow chart of preparation, characterization and application of MVO.	44
Figure 3.2	Flow chart of the hydrothermal method for the preparation of MVO.	45
Figure 3.3	The Stainless steel autoclave used for the synthesis of MVO during the hydrothermal method.	46
Figure 3.4	Schematic diagram for absorption spectra using Uv/visible spectrometer for different dyes.	47
Figure 3.5	Purposed Schematic mechanism Electrochemical CHI-760 analyzer for the Bio-sensor application.	48
Figure 3.6	Schematic illustration for the hydrothermal growth of BiVO$_4$.	49
Figure 3.7	Purposed synthesis procedure for the preparation of FeVO$_4$.nanoparticles.	50
Figure 3.8	Growth procedure for the synthesis of Zn$_3$(VO$_4$)$_2$ nanoplates.	51
Figure 3.9	Flow chart of the hydrothermal method for the preparation of BiVO$_4$/FeVO$_4$.	53

Figure 3.10	Nanomaterials characterization techniques. (a) X-ray diffraction (XRD), (b) Energy dispersive X-ray spectroscopy (EDS), (c) Scanning electron microscopy (SEM), (d) Fourier transform infrared spectroscopy (FTIR), (e) Raman spectroscopy (f) X-ray photoelectron spectroscopy (XPS), (g) Photo luminance spectroscopy (PL), (h)Brunauer-Emmett-Teller (BET) surface area analyzer and (i)Electronic paramagnetic Resonance (ESR) spectroscopy.	55
Figure 4.1.1	The XRD pattern for the as-synthesized $BiVO_4$ nanoparticles.	57
Figure 4.1.2	(a) SEM image at magnification (X75000) (b) TEM image of $BiVO_4$ nanoparticles (c) EDX pattern of $BiVO_4$ synthesized by hydrothermal method at 180 °C.	58
Figure 4.1.3	FT-IR spectrum of m-$BiVO_4$ synthesised by hydrothermal method at 180°C.	58
Figure 4.1.4	Nitrogen adsorption-desorption analysis of m-$BiVO_4$ and pore diameter (inset) by Brunauer-Emmet-Teller.	59
Figure 4.1.5	(a) Photocatalytic degradation of Rhodamine-B (RhB), in inset UV-visible badgap calculated by Tauc plot method (b) Photocatalytic degradation of Crystal Violet (CV).	60
Figure 4.1.6	(a) Degradation efficiency of $BiVO_4$ nanoparticles and (b) Photocatalytic degradation analysis by using Pseudo first order equation.	61
Figure 4.1.7	PL emission spectra of m-$BiVO_4$ at room temperature.	63
Figure 4.2.1	SEM images of the as-synthesized $FeVO_4$ nanoparticles at (a) 2μm, 200 KX magnification; (b) 200nm, 20000 KX magnification; (c) 200nm, 29000 KX magnification and (d) 200nm 30000 KX magnification.	67
Figure 4.2.2	Energy dispersive analysis of the $FeVO_4$ nanoparticles.	69
Figure 4.2.3	XRD pattern of the $FeVO_4$ obtained at 180 °C for 24 h with the pH ~8.	68

Figure 4.2.4	FTIR spectrum of FeVO$_4$ nanoparticles synthesis at 180°C for 24 hr and pH ~8	69
Figure 4.2.5	Structure of Methylene blue (MB) used as sample dye.	69
Figure 4.2.6	**(a)** Photocatalytic degradation of methylene blue (MB) dye when 0.05 ml of reaction initiator (H$_2$O$_2$) is used **(b)** photocatalytic degradation efficiency of NP's **(c)** Degradation concentration C/C$_0$ analysis.	71
Figure 4.2.7	(a) shows the BET specific surface area of FeVO$_4$ from nitrogen adsorption-desorption curve **(b)** differential pore size distribution curve from Barret-Joyner-Halender (BJH) method **(c)** Band gap calculated by Tauc's plot method.	71
Figure 4.2.8	**(a)** Photocatalytic degradation of methylene blue (MB) dye when 0.2 ml of reaction initiator (H2O2) is used **(b)** photocatalytic degradation efficiency of NP's **(c)** Degradation analysis.	72
Figure 4.2.9	**(a)** Photocatalytic degradation of methylene blue (MB) dye when 0.3 ml of reaction initiator (H2O2) is used **(b)** photocatalytic degradation efficiency of NP's **(c)** Degradation analysis.	73
Figure 4.2.10	**(a)** shows the BET specific surface area of FeVO$_4$ from nitrogen adsorption-desorption curve **(b)** differential pore size distribution curve from Barret-Joyner-Halender (BJH) method **(c)** Band gap calculated by Tauc's plot method.	74
Figure 4.2.11	PL spectrum of FeVO$_4$ nanoparticles at room temperature.	75
Figure 4.2.12	Effect of the initial dye concentration on photocatalytic degradation of MB.	76
Figure 4.2.13	Stability curves of the photocatalyst FeVO$_4$ for degradation of MB dye.	77
Figure 4.2.14	Uv-visible spectra of real waste water sample.	77
Figure 4.3.1	SEM image at low magnification, and high magnification of Zn$_3$(VO$_4$)$_2$ nanoplates hydrothermally synthesized at 180°C.	80
Figure 4.3.2	EDX analysis of Zn$_3$(VO$_4$)$_2$ nanoplates synthesis at 180°C.	80

Figure 4.3.3	The XRD pattern for the as-synthesized $Zn_3(VO_4)_2$ nanoplates at 180 °C.	81
Figure 4.3.4	(a) wide scan total XPS spectrum of the $Zn_3(VO_4)_2$ nanoplates sample, (b) ForZn 2p; (c) For V 2p and (d) For O 1s.	82
Figure 4.3.5	FTIR spectrum of the as-prepared $Zn_3(VO_4)_2$ nanoplates.	83
Figure 4.3.6	Photocatalysis mechanism for the degradation of dyes.	84
Figure 4.3.7	(a) Nitrogen adsorption-desorption curve for surface area measurement of $Zn_3(VO_4)_2$ nanoplates (b)Tauc plot for $Zn_3(VO_4)_2$ composite.	85
Figure 4.3.8	Chemical Structure of Congo red (CR) and Crystal Violet (CV) dyes.	86
Figure 4.3.9	(a) Absorption bands of CR solution at illuminated times taking 50mL CR solution under visible light, (b) CR concentration ratio treated with ZnVO-Nps solution at different irradiation time, (c) Error bar graph for photocatalytic measurement of CR solution.	87
Figure 4.3.10	(a) Absorption spectra of CV solution at different interval carrying 10mL CV solution under visible light, (b) CV concentration ratio treated with ZnVO-Nps solution at different irradiation time, (c) Error bar graph for photocatalytic measurement of CV solution.	87
Figure 4.3.11	Photoluminescence (PL) spectrum of ZnVO-Nps at room temperature	88
Figure 4.4.1	(a) XRD spectrum of $BiVO_4$/$FeVO_4$ composite heterojunction photocatalyst at different mole ratio 1:5, 1:2, 1:1, 2:1, 5:1 and 10:1; (b) Peaks shifts in the XRD spectrum of $BiVO_4$/$FeVO_4$ by increasing concentration of $BiVO_4$ (c) EDS analysis of $BiVO_4$/$FeVO_4$ composite at mole ratio 2:1.	92
Figure 4.4.2	SEM images of $BiVO_4$/$FeVO_4$ composite heterojunction photocatalyst at different mole ratio (a) 1:5, (b) 1:2, (c) 1:1, (d) 2:1, (e) 5:1 and (f) 10:1.	93

Figure 4.4.3	XPS of BiVO$_4$/FeVO$_4$ nanocomposite at different mole ratios of BiVO$_4$ and FeVO$_4$.	94
Figure 4.4.4	BET surface area (inset pore diameter) of 2:1 BiVO$_4$/FeVO$_4$ composite at 77.35 K.	95
Figure 4.4.5	Show the N$_2$ gas isotherms at 77.5 K of BiVO$_4$/FeVO$_4$ nanocomposite at a different mole ratio at (a) 1:5 (b) 1:2 (c) 1:1 (d) 5:1 and (e) 10:1 the BET surface area and BJH pore size in inset.	96
Figure 4.4.6	(a) FT-IR spectra and (b) Raman spectra of the BiVO4/FeVO4 heterogeneous composites prepared with different molar ratios.	97
Figure 4.4.7	The photocatalytic degradation of Crystal violet dye by FeVO$_4$, BiVO$_4$ and BiVO$_4$/FeVO$_4$ hetro junction anophotocatalyst at (a) Pure FeVO$_4$, (b) 1:5, (c) 1:2, (d) 1:1, (e) 2:1, (f) 5:1, (g) 10:1 mole ratio and (h) Pure BiVO$_4$.	99
Figure 4.4.8	(a) Concentration changes of CV dye as a function of irradiation time using FeVO4, BiVO4 and BiVO4/FeVO4 at molar ratios of 1 : 5, 1 : 2, 1 : 1, 2 : 1, 5 : 1 and 10 : 1. (b) Degradation error bar profile of CV over BiVO4/FeVO4 at different molar ratios as a function of time. (c)Tauc plot for BiVO4/FeVO4 composite with a 2: 1 ratio.	100
Figure 4.4.9	Reaction mechanism of crystal violet photodegradation over BiVO$_4$/FeVO$_4$ composite under the visible light.	102
Figure 4.4.10	DMPO spin trapping EPR spectra for DMPO- ˙O$_2^-$ and DMPO- ˙OH$^-$ in visible light irradiation with BiVO$_4$/FeVO$_4$ photocatalyst.	103
Figure 4.4.11	(a) Absorption spectra of CV solution at different concentration of BiVO$_4$/FeVO$_4$ in 10mL CV solution, for 1h respectively. (b) Effect of the initial dye concentration on photocatalytic degradation of CV (c) Stability curves of the BiVO$_4$/FeVO$_4$ photocatalyst for CV dye under visible light.	104
Figure 4.4.12	PL spectra of the BiVO$_4$/FeVO$_4$ composites at different concentrations.	105

Figure 4.4.13	Electrochemical Impedance spectroscopy of bare and modified BiVO4/FeVO4 nanocomposite GCE in different electrolytes **(a)** 0.1 M H3PO4, **(b)** 0.1 M Li2SO4, **(c)** 0.1 M NaSO4 and **(d)** 0.1 M of NaOH.	106
Figure 4.4.14	CVs of the BiVO4/FeVO4 modified GCE in **(a)** 0.1 M H_3PO_4, **(b)** 0.1 M Li_2SO_4, **(c)** 0.1 M $NaSO_4$ and **(d)** 0.1 M of NaOH solution in the absence and presence of 0.5 mM ascorbic acid, Scan rate 50 mVs^{-1}.	107
Figure 4.4.15	CVs of the BiVO$_4$/FeVO$_4$ modified GCE in mixed **(a)** 0.1 M H$_3$PO$_4$, **(b)** 0.1 M Li$_2$SO$_4$, **(c)** 0.1 M NaSO$_4$, **(d)** 0.1 M of NaOH and Ascorbic acid (0.5mM) solution Scan rate 50 mVs^{-1}, recycling for 1st and 20th time.	108
Figure 4.5.1	XRD spectrum of $Zn_3(VO_4)_2$/BiVO$_4$ heterojunction composite at different mole ratio **(a)** 5:1, **(b)** 2:1, **(c)** 1:1, **(d)** 1:5, and **(e)** 1:10	110
Figure 4.5.2	SEM images of $Zn_3(VO_4)_2$/BiVO$_4$ composite heterojunction photocatalyst at different mole ratio **(a)** 5:1, **(b)** 2:1, **(c)** 1:1, **(d)** 1:5, **(e)** 1:10 and **(f)** EDS analysis of $Zn_3(VO_4)_2$/BiVO$_4$ composite at mole ratio 1:1.	111
Figure 4.5.3	UV-vis absorption spectra of Methylene blue dye for different irradiation times showing photocatalytic degradation of Methylene blue dye through $Zn_3(VO_4)_2$/BiVO$_4$ heterogeneous nano photocatalyst at mole ratio **(a)** 5:1, **(b)** 2:1, **(c)** 1:1, **(d)** 1:5, **(e)** 1:10 and **(f)** Efficiency of MB dye as a function of irradiation time in the presence of photocatalyst at same quantity but different mole ratios.	112
Figure 4.5.4	**(a)** N2 adsorption–desorption isotherm distribution curves for $Zn_3(VO_4)_2$/BiVO$_4$ at 2:1 mole ratio, inset (i) differential pore size distribution curve from Barret-Joyner-Halender (BJH) method (ii) high resolution N_2 adsorption–desorption isotherm at 2:1 mole ratio **(b)** Tauc plot for $Zn_3(VO_4)_2$/BiVO$_4$composite at 2:1 mole	113

ratio.

Figure 4.5.5	(a) Concentration changes (C/C$_o$) of MB dye as a function of irradiation time in the presence of photocatalyst at same quantity but different mole ratios (b) bar graph of efficiency at different mole ratios.	115
Figure 4.5.6	UV-vis absorption spectra of Methylene blue dye for different irradiation times showing photocatalytic degradation of Methylene blue dye using Zn$_3$(VO$_4$)$_2$/BiVO$_4$ heterogeneous nano photocatalyst at pH (a) 2, (b) 5, (c) 7, (d) 10, (e) 12, and (f) Efficiency of MB dye as a function of irradiation time at different pH values in the presence of photocatalyst.	116
Figure 4.5.7	(a) Concentration changes (C/Co) of MB dye as a function of irradiation time in the presence of photocatalyst at different pH (b) bar graph of Efficiency of Zn$_3$(VO$_4$)$_2$/BiVO$_4$ nanophotocatalyst at different pH values.	117
Figure 4.5.8	(a) PL spectra of Zn$_3$(VO$_4$)$_2$/BiVO$_4$ composite at different concentrations (b) stability of Zn$_3$(VO$_4$)$_2$/BiVO$_4$ for degradation of Methyl blue dye under visible light.	118
Figure 4.5.9	DMPO spin trapping EPR spectra for DMPO−$^{\bullet}$O$_2^-$ and DMPO−$^{\bullet}$OH$^-$ in visible light irradiation with Zn$_3$(VO$_4$)$_2$/BiVO$_4$ photocatalyst.	119
Figure 4.5.10	Electrochemical Impedance spectroscopy of bare and modified Zn$_3$(VO$_4$)$_2$/BiVO$_4$ nanocomposite GCE in different electrolytes (a) 0.1 M Li$_2$SO$_4$, (b) 0.1 M MgSO$_4$, (c) 0.1 M KOH and (d) 0.1 M of NaOH.	121
Figure 4.5.11	CVs of the Zn$_3$(VO$_4$)$_2$/BiVO$_4$ modified GCE in (a) 0.1 M Li$_2$SO$_4$, (b) 0.1 M MgSO$_4$, (c) 0.1 M of KOH and (d) 0.1 M of NaOH solution in the absence and presence of 0.5 mM Hydrogen peroxide at scan rate: 50 mV s^{-1}.	123

Figure 4.5.12 CVs of the $Zn_3(VO_4)_2$/$BiVO_4$ modified GCE in mixed **(a)** 0.1 M LiSO4 **(b)** 0.1 M MgSO4, **(c)** 0.1 M KOH, **(d)** 0.1 M of NaOH and Hydrogen peroxide (0.5mM) solution Scan rate: 50 mV s^{-1}, recycling for 1st and 20th time. ... 124

THE LIST OF TABLES

Table 3.1	Shows the various materials and chemicals, the detailed of the suppliers are also provided for references.	42
Table 4.1	X-ray diffraction intensities and preferred growth orientation factor for $BiVO_4$	56
Table 4.2	Comparison of Photocatalytic activity of some previous reported photocatalysts and present $BiVO_4$ for degradation of Rhodamine-B (RhB) and Crystal violet (CV).	63
Table 4.3	Comparison of Photocatalytic activity of some previous reported photocatalysts and present $FeVO_4$ Methylene blue (MB) under visible light irradiation.	78
Table 4.4	Comparison of Photocatalytic activity of some photocatalysts and Current $Zn_3(VO_4)_2$ for degradation of CR and CV dye under visible light irradiation.	90
Table 4.5	The degradation comparison of Methylene blue dye using the $Zn_3(VO_4)_2/BiVO_4$ composite with other nanomaterial photocatalysts.	120

ABSTRACT

Nowadays there is a continuously increasing worldwide concern for organicmicro pollutants such as antibiotics, personal care products, plasticizers, surfactants, herbicides, etc., because they generate significant environmental problems. Unfortunately, conventional waste water treatment techniques can not completely remove all residues of these emerging contaminants. In this context, the development of nanotechnology in the sector of Advance oxidation process (AOP) Photocatalysis creates opportunities for environmental cleanup at relatively lower costs. In this study metal vanadate based nanostructures namely; bismuth vanadate ($BiVO_4$), ferric vanadate ($FeVO_4$), zinc vanadate $Zn_3(VO_4)_2$, bismuth vanadate/ferric vanadate ($BiVO_4/FeVO_4$) and zinc vanadate/bismuth vanadate ($Zn_3(VO_4)_2/BiVO_4$) were fabricated by using facile hydrothermal route. The possible reaction processes of the as-synthesized nanomaterials were discussed briefly. Optimizations of the growth and/or synthesis conditions were performed to obtainhigh quality metal vanadate nanostructures (nanoparticles, nano-plates, nanorods and nano-flowers). Parameters which affect the activity of the photo catalysts, namely, the amount of molar ratio, catalyst loading, pH, heating time and reaction temperature were also studied extensively. Characterization of the nanostructures were performed by powder X-ray diffraction (XRD), Scanning electron microscopy (SEM), energy dispersive spectroscopy (EDX), X-rays photoelectron microscopy (XPS), UV (ultraviolet) spectrophotometer, Fourier transform infrared spectroscopy (FTIR),Transmission electron microscopy (TEM), Raman Spectroscopy, Brunauer–Emmett–Teller (BET) surface area analyzer, photoluminance (PL), electron paramagnetic resonance (EPR) spectrophotometer. For catalytic response the as prepared samples were used to degrade the different pollutants organic dyes (crystal violet (CV), methylene blue (MB), congo red (CR), Rhodamine-B (RhB)) and industrial waste water, electrochemical response of ($BiVO_4/FeVO_4$) and ($Zn_3(VO_4)_2/BiVO_4$) over ascorbic acid (A.A) and hydrogen peroxide (H_2O_2) was evaluated by using electrochemical impedance spectroscopy (EIS) and cyclic voltammetry (CV) techniques. The as-prepared metal vanadate nanomaterials exhibited excellent photocatalytic response for dye solutions, industrial waste water and sensors

CHAPTER 1

INTRODUCTION

1.1 Background and Motivation

Clean water is vital natural assets for all God's creatures (Human being, animals and plants) in the world. The excessive population crowdedness and at the same height of industrialization generate substantial environmental challenges all over the world. The high polluting materials (inorganic and organic) specified as antibiotics, personal care products, plasticisers, wetting agent, and herbicides give birth to environmental complications. Antibiotics may have adverse effects on aquatic life as they are incompletely metabolized by the body. A considerable portion of these substances is usually excreted in their pharmacologically active forms and ends up in the sewage system. Due to their continuous release from anthropogenic sources into the environment during the last decade and limited biodegradability, they now comprise a new group of water contaminants of increasing national and global concern. Unfortunately, conventional wastewater treatment techniques cannot completely remove or destroy residues of these emerging contaminants. In this context, the development of nanotechnology for environmental cleanup creates opportunities. Nanotechnology may provide unique and economical skills for remediation of such pollutants by catalytic demolition and adsorption (Zhao et al., 2011). Nanotechnology refers to the use of matter with at least one dimension below 100 nanometers. Such materials can exhibit unique properties for various applications. Currently, significant development has been prepared to fabricate shape organized nanoparticles, such as nanorods and nanowires, particularly using chemical synthesis methods. The overall goal is to improve the working and usage of nanomaterials in favour of various applications, vary between sensing devices to photonic materials, electronic engineering and enhanced oxidation techniques. Significant advancement has been made over the past decade in the preparation of monodispersed nanoparticles with controllable composition and structure. Among these, inorganic nanoparticles with controlled outlines are the favourably encouraging candidates for building blocks in nanostructures and nanodevices. This is due to both substantial change in their physical properties as related to a sphere-shaped nanoparticles and their intrinsic array providing a number of innovative probabilities against gathering in organized structures. For example, elongated and a rod formed nano crystalstrain incredible physical stuff, resulting in unique activity in photocatalysis, light emitting devices, optically brought light inflexion, and photovoltaic, etc (Krahne et al., 2011). Many researches conveyed the exploit of semiconductor photocatalysts for solar energy transformation and environmental clearance. In environmental remediation, they may contribute to minimizing the use of energy for pollution control. Among the available photocatalysts, ZnO and TiO_2 are the most promising because of high oxidizing ability and minimal toxicity to the environment. However, their relatively low general quantum effectiveness produced by the excessive recombination level of photo-induced charge pairs by the side of or neighbouring their surface, is one of the main drawbacks. The rate of electron-hole pair recombination can be suppressed in several ways, for instance, by applying Nano-sized crystallites as an alternative of bulk ingredients or by varying photocatalysts by doping them with ions, sensitizing nanoparticles with dye molecules, and forming composite nanoparticles with appropriate band gaps (Liqiang et al., 2006).

In the present study metal vanadate based nanomaterials were prepared and studied for photocatalysis and electrochemical sensing related application. The photocatalytic response of the nanomaterials were investigated for model dyes and decontamination of industrial wastewater, whereas, electrochemical behavior was studied for the detection and sensing of different analytes.

1.2 Nanotechnology

The term "Nano" have in mind dwarf in the Greek language. It is Used as a prefix on behalf of any unit like a meter or a second and it means a billionth part of that unit ($1nm = 10^{-9}$). Nanotechnology is termed as a skill where sizes and acceptances in the range of 0.1– 100nm play a vital role (Goyal et al., 2010; Radad et al., 2012). Nanotechnology ranging is enormously different, from conventional device to completely new complex line of attack based upon the molecular self-reliant unit. One nanometer is usually looked at attentively a magical point on the scale. This is so because there is a change in a short space of time in all the properties of a material when it just enters into the nanoscale i.e. <100nm. The justification for this change is the sudden becoming apparent for some of the basic interactions in the middle atoms that are averaged out of existence in the bulk material (Ghosh Chaudhuri et al., 2011).

1.2.1 Background

Nanotechnology is the concept and engagement of materials and devices of development of the semiconductor microelectronic revolution which originally call forth the evolution of micro-electrochemical systems. The commercial needs of electronic manufacturers and biological applications have yielded the necessity to produce, realized and ensure physical object on ever-smaller scales, therefore giving an impulse to investigators to bob up with novel ideas. To entirely benefit from the rewards provided by nanotechnology, it is significant to understand how to build analyses and prefigure the properties of these nanoscopic things (Kim et al., 2003; J. Zhang et al., 2009).

Historically, the first use of the concepts found in nanotechnology was made by physicist Richard Feynman in his impressive lecture "There's Plenty of Room at the Bottom" delivered at Caltech on 29 December 1959. The word "Nanotechnology" was created by Professor Norio Taniguchi (Tokyo University of Sciences) in his paper in 1974 in the following words: "Nanotechnology" generally comprises of the treating of, split-up, amalgamation and twist of materials by one atom or by one molecule." Dr. K Eric Drexler promoted the word through his book (Engine of Creation and Nanosystems). Nanotechnology brings into being in the 1980s, predominantly owing to the development of assembling discipline and the establishment of the scanning tunnelling microscope (STM).Its advancement has also facilitated the improvement of SemiconductorNanocrystals. Thus, nanotechnology is a multidisciplinary subject, bringing untidily physicists, chemists, biologists, and engineers to investigate this unique field (Shchukin et al., 2013; Sivakumar et al., 2011).

1.2.2 Why work on the Nanoscale?

The possessions of bulk resources are commonly well understood. On the other hand, as the size of a Particle decreased to nano-regime (1-100nm) results in different characters. The property of the material is determined by the space available for the electrons to execute their characteristic motion. Therefore, the changes in physicochemical properties are observed as the size and shape changes. Along with the physicochemical attributes, there exists a remarkable deal of fascination in terms of the applications in nanotechnology. It has been estimated that the nanotech industry could be worth up to $1 trillion in the next 10-20 years (Roco, 2017).

1.2.3 Nanomaterials

Nanomaterials stand for a field that precedes materials discipline centred approach to nanotechnology. Materials with at least one representative dimension range between 1-100nm known as nanomaterials. Properties of Nanomaterials can be different from those of the same materials with bulk or mm-scale dimensions. Nanomaterials, the building blocks of nanotechnology, can be engineered physically and chemically for specific applications. Regarding dimension, nanomaterials can be divided into four categories as 1) zero-dimensional materials, such as nanoparticles, Powders; 2) on the 1-D nanomaterials, i.e nanotubes, nanowires, etc.; 3) 2-D nanomaterials, i.e thin films, quantum wells, nanosheets and 4) three-dimensional quantum dots, nanospheres. The novel properties of nanomaterials can be divided into two primary categories such as surface area and quantum confinement effects. In explaining the change in surface-related effects properties is to take into consideration the increase in surface area to volume ratio as we go to smaller particle sizes. The greater the surface for the same volume, the greater is the reactivity. The physical and chemical reactivity of the element changes at nanoscale due to the increase in surface area. Nanoscale structures may possess change in physical properties like band gap, melting point etc (Choy, 2003; Weisbuch et al., 2014).

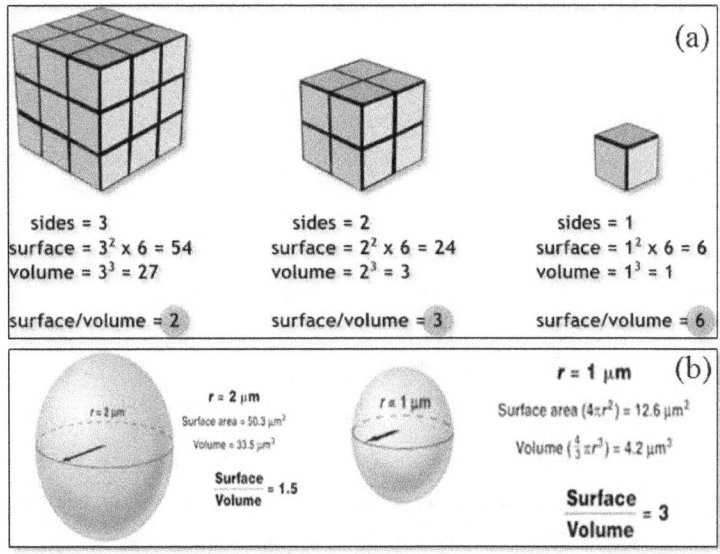

Figure 1.1: (a) and (b) Illustration the increase in surface area to volume ratio.

A quantum effect occurs when the wavelength of an electron in a material comprises of as is order as a dimension of the material. This restricts the movement of an electron in the material, which goes quantized in that confining dimension. The density of states of the electrons are so checked by the numeral of dimensions in which electrons are quantized (Weisbuch & Vinter, 2014). In addition, several physical properties variation while compared to macroscopic systems. Quantum confinement is careful with the setup of energy dissimilarity surrounded by states and energy band gap. Particle performances as it remained free when the sizes are enormous than the wavelength of the particle. In this position, the band gap remains at real template energy due to a continuous energy state. On the other hand, when the restricting dimensions shrinkages at a particular limit, on average in nanoscale, the energy goes to discrete spectrum. Consequently, the band gap converts dimension dependent. This finally an upshot in a blue shift in optical enlightenment as the dimension of the particle reduces.

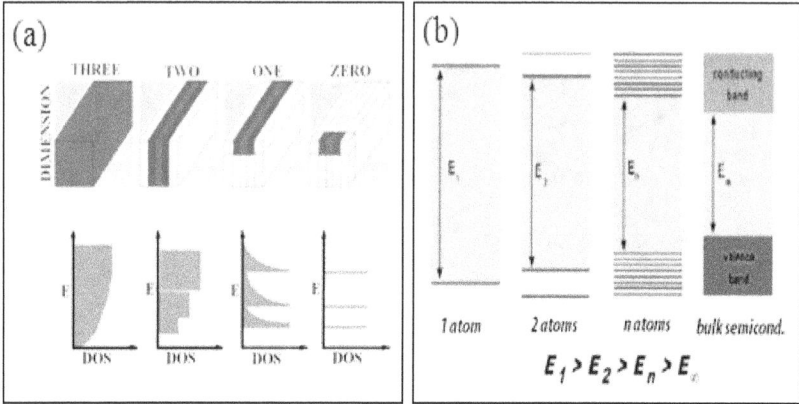

Figure 1.2: (a) A schematic diagram illustrating the changes in electronic density of states that occur as dimensionality is varied from 3D to 0D, assuming free electrons **(b)** Quantum confinement is mature for the intensification of energy difference between energy states and bandgap. (Waheed S. Khan, 2011)

Two diverse approaches exercised in nanotechnology toward the fabrication of nanostructures stated as "top-down" and "bottom-up"(Samuelson, 2003). These terms were used to the field by Dr. K Eric Drexler in 1989. Top-down stands for standard microfabrication approaches with deposition, etching and ion beam milling on substrates in order to reduce the adjacent dimensions to the nanometer extent. In the top-down approach substantially well-ordered nanostructures can be achieved, on the other hand at the instant this technology does not bring about the industrial requirements for the fabrication of little price tag and large quantities of devices. Moreover, the one-dimensional nanostructures manufactured with these techniques are not single-crystalline generally. Bottom-up be made up of the get-together of molecular building blocks. The bottom-up approach lets little cost manufacture even if it is difficult to develop them well regular and periodic. Moreover, further regulator and understanding into the growth treat be attained for their product integration in functional devices (Hanrath et al., 2002).

1.3 Hydrothermal Crystal Growth Technology

A hydrothermal synthesis is a special case of a solvothermal method that is usually well-defined as a chemical reaction proceeding in a solvent at temperatures above the diluter highpoint and at pressures exceeding 1 bar. The medium used in a solvothermal synthesis can thus be anything from water hydrothermal to ammonia and alcohol or any other organic or inorganic solvent. The hydrothermal method adventures that by increasing temperature and pressures the fundamental properties of water and its capabilities as a solvent changes that produces significant characteristics and as a result different parameter can be set to achieve desired crystal.

1.3.1 Background

Hydrothermal synthesis method was discovery a geologist of British, Sir Roderick Impey Murchisin in 1849, he claimed the exploit of water at high temperature and pressure is capable of the exchanges in the earth's crust principally to the creation of dissimilar rocks and minerals.

1.3.2 Reactors for Hydrothermal Synthesis

An orthodox hydrothermal synthesis is performed in a batch reactor the precursors are simply dissolved or suspended in water in an autoclave which can endure high temperatures and pressures The autoclave is subsequently sealed and heated to the desired temperature while the pressure is most often autogenously generated depending on the degree of autoclave filling pressures of up several hundred bars can be obtained even at low temperatures. The autoclave sketched in Figure 1.3 is typical lab scale version as is also used at Government College University Faisalabad (GCUF), Pakistan; lab simply consists of a Teflon cup inserted in a steel shell which can be sealed with a steel lid.

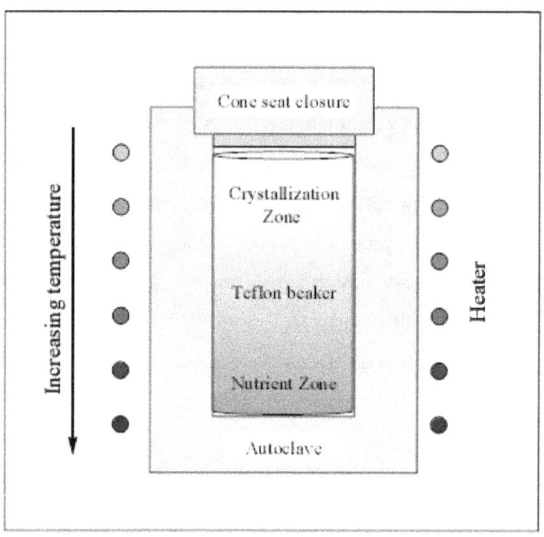

Figure 1.3: Schematic drawing of Experimental autoclave apparatus for hydrothermal crystal growth.

1.4 Vanadium

Vanadium was initially exposed in a Mexican lead ore in 1801, Andres Manuel del Rio the Spanish mineralogist, who named the new element Erythronium (Wong et al.) even rather than Dalton's atomic hypothesis (1803-1808). However, in 1805, H.V. Collet-Descotils, the French chemist speciously deduced that this fresh component was only impure chromium and brown ore was a basic lead chromate. Far ahead, the Swedish chemist Nils Gabriel Sefstrom, in 1830, rediscovered the element from models of iron melted as of an excavate in Sweden and named it vanadium after Vanadis, the Old Norse name for the Scandinavian goddess stand for the goddess of beauty, for the richness and diversity of colours of its composites. In 1831, Sefstrom, J. J. Berzelius and Friedrich Wohler established unambiguously the chemical individuality of vanadium and its characteristics with del Rio's Erythronium (Rejniak et al.). Vanadium is found in approximately 152 diverse raw materials amongst which the significant ones are patronite, vanadinite, roscoelite, and carnotite. It is in some of the greatest abundant and comprehensively spread metals in the earth's crust. The main sources of vanadium are present in titaniferrous magnetite ores from mines in Australia, China, Russia and South Africa. Considerable of the vanadium metal existence manufactured by calcium reduction of vanadium pentoxide in a pressurized container, an adaption of a process developed by McKechnie and Seybair. The annual world production of vanadium is about 38,000 tonnes and almost 80% of this is used as ferrovanadium or as a steel additive. Vanadium Compounds are expended in the aerospace industry also, e.g. titanium– aluminium– vanadium Alloys for aero-engine gas turbines and underneath carriages of planes. Vanadium is also used in porcelains, semiconductor technology, dyes for textiles and leather (Thomas, 1994; Weckhuysen et al., 2003). Vanadium as Catalysts also performs Corrosion of methanol to formaldehyde and to methyl formate and toluene to benzaldehyde, (V- Ti-O catalysts), oxidation of polycyclic aromatic hydrocarbons, for example, phenanthrene, anthracene, fluorene, and naphthalene to carboxylic acids and quinones (V-Fe-O system). Vanadium containing systems are used not only for the production of important compounds on the other hand also for the reduction of environmental toxic waste. Fig. 1.4: Indication of the significance of vanadium is maintained metal oxide catalysis. The facts are highlighted on open texts search in the era 1967–2000 (Burcham et al., 1999; Concepcion et al., 1999; Hadjiivanov et al., 2000; Kortüm et al., 1963; Kubelka et al., 1931).

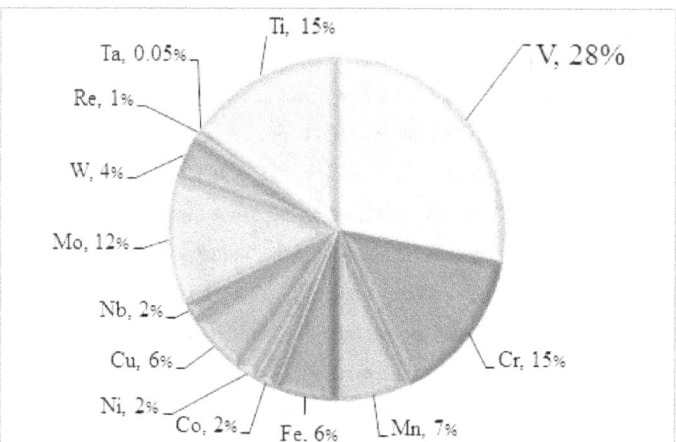

Figure 1.4: Reviews the number of papers (percentage of the total amount of papers) of numerous transition metals in the area of material catalysis, which is able to be retrieved in the open literature. The fact that the highest number of papers is published on the vanadium-based catalysts underlines the importance of vanadium in supported metal oxide catalysis.

1.4.1 Ammonium Metavanadate, NH_4VO_3

Ammonium Metavanadate, $NH4VO3$, is one of the typical sources of vanadium, operated as a starting agent for the manufacture of vanadium salts.

$$NH_4VO_3 \text{ (s)} = V_2O_5 \text{ (s)} + 2NH_3 \text{ (g)} + H_2O \text{ (l)} - 43,600 \text{ (Cal)}.$$

At above 210°C temperatures, the salts goes through diminution and provide a rest of the minimal vanadate, and might besides provide various nitrides.

1.5 Statement of the problem

A recent scientific studies urge that vanadium would have excellent photocatalytic activities that may be useful for degradation of organic micropollutants as titanium dioxide nanoparticles do, but in addition, it also showed a photo memory/recyclability effect (Liu et al., 2015; Seliverstov et al., 2014). Among the existing short bandgap (<3 eV) photocatalysis, vanadate is expected to work for productive photocatalysis. The report on uses of vanadium oxide in electrochemical devices is considerably more than its practice as a heterogeneous photocatalyst.

According to literature survey few articles have been reported in the literature for vanadate as a prospective photocatalyst to decompose toxic environmental contaminants (Lee et al., 2008). Perhaps, the slight vanadate solubility in the solution is the main argument which queries its suitability as water refining photocatalyst.

The main focus of study/dissertation relies on the investigation of metal vanadate based nanomaterials (Bismuth Vanadate, Zinc Vanadate and Ferric Vanadate) as a potential new catalyst for decomposition of organic micropollutants and electrochemical sensing of analytes. We studied the photocatalytic activity as well as bio-sensing application of the metal vanadate nanomaterials. Hydrothermal route is adopted for the synthesis of materials. This method was chosen for the reason that it has several merits like low price, low energy depletion, and uncomplicated apparatus needs. It is a naturally non-threatening and environmental friendly technology as the results come to pass in closed scheme circumstances where water is used asa reaction agent.

1.6 The objective of the study

The objectives of this study were to prepare metal vanadate based high quality (Bismuth vanadate, Zinc vanadate and ferric vanadate) nanomaterials and explore their potential use in environmental remediation and electrochemical bio-sensor field. Particularly, the study aimed to:

1) Study effects of some parameters that may affect the size (diameter and length), shape (spherical, rod, etc.), and surface area of nanoparticles during chemical syntheses, like temperature, pH and reaction time,
2) Characterize the produced metal vanadate based nanomaterials, and
3) Evaluate the photocatalytic activity of the produced vanadate based nanomaterials
4) Electrochemical behaviour was studied for the detection and sensing of different analytes.

CHAPTER 2
REVIEW OF LITERATURE

Tremendous research work has been performed for the nanostructures; here some of the work will be cited as review.

2.1 Nanostructures

(Morose, 2010) Intend to look at several factors Can affect the properties of nanostructures, among these, size (diameter, length, width, etc.), Colour, conduction, melting point and reactivity. For instance, the melting point for gold with a span of 6nm is 1150 K approximately doubles the melting temperature 650 K for gold with a span of 2 nm.

(Radad et al., 2012) Investigated the term nanoparticle (NP) refers to particles with sizes between 1 and 100nm that show extraordinary properties compared to the corresponding micro materials. The reason is that nanostructures materials obligate a well-built surface area to volume ratio. As for the size of nanoparticle shrinkages, the small percentage of surface atoms upturns, as a result, it increases the response and sorts them well responsive catalysts.

(Prasad et al., 2013) Nanomaterials form a recent area of intense scientific interest because Nano scale materials exhibit unique properties and have extensive variability of applications in the growth technology of magnetic materials for data storage, optoelectronics, medical diagnostics, photocatalysis, sensors, and alternative energy.

(Ferreira et al., 2013) Investigated Potential applications of nano technologies have been investigated in some important sectors, such as energy, transport network, water decontamination, contamination reduction and Environmental improvement, medical and biomedical applications. This technology allows Significant reduction of resource consumption and pollution via improving the sustainability of energy utilization, Recycling and Detoxification technology.

2.1.1 Types of nanostructures

(Schoiswohl et al., 2006) reported that there are four forms of Nanomaterials built on their dimensionality, these are 0D -Nano clusters, 1D layer, 2D -Nano-grained coatings, and 3D- bulk objects. One-dimensional nano structures (1D), such as Nano rods, nanowires, nanotubes, and Nano belts have inspired material scientists recently due to their exceptional Optical, electronic and automated properties and their possible placations in both fundamental research and fabricating Nano devices.

(Ju-Nam et al., 2008) Investigated On the basis of chemical composition, nanostructures are categorized as carbon based nanomaterials and inorganic materials. Inorganic nanoparticles are extra classified as metallic oxides (ZnO, FeO, TeO, etc), metals (Au, Ag, Fe, etc) and quantum dots (CdS, CdSe, etc).

(Gao et al., 2008) presented at the same time efforts are going on to guide these 1D nanostructures into 2D or 3D configurations, as this is an inevitable step for the fabrication of nano devices and would carry novel morphology and applications that outcome from the three- dimensional location and agreement of the nano crystals.

(Radad et al., 2012) reported that Nanoparticles are classified as engineered nanoparticles (ENPs) and non-engineered nanoparticles (NENPs). Engineered NPs are manufactured with intent for certain purposes. On the other hand, non-engineered nanoparticles are developed in unwanted behaviours for example particles produced as a side effect, in the case of fuels combustion.

2.1.2 Synthesis of nanostructures

(Thakkar et al., 2010) reported that size reduction may involve various physical and chemical treatments, such as for mechanical crushing, chemical etching, laser and thermal ablation. The major drawback of the "top-down" method is the introduction of imperfections in the surface structure of the product. For the ''bottom-up'' synthesis, the nanostructure should be arranged atom-by- atom, layer-by-layer to build the nanoscale structures from Their atomic and molecular constituents either by chemical or biological procedures.

(Ahmed et al., 2011) reported, in the photocatalytic deprivation of carbon built contaminations, the decreasing procedure of oxygen and the oxidation of impurities should carry on at the same rate. Otherwise, it will cause accumulation of electrons in the CB (usually if there is no Sufficient oxygen in the solution), thereby increasing the rate of the recombination of an e-h and delaying the photocatalytic oxidation process. Nevertheless, photocatalytic activities highly rely on the intrinsic properties of catalyst like crystal structure, surface capacity, particle extent spreading, absorbency, superficial hydroxyl thickness and band gap of the photo catalysts.

(Krystek et al., 2011) examine that these methods can generally be categorized as "top-down" and "bottom-up. In top-down approach the manufacture of nanostructured materials by size reduction of a very big solid material into smaller, nano-sized portions, from a suitable starting material.

(Kango et al., 2013) discovered that Nano structures may be manufactured by various beginning materials by Altered physical and chemical approaches, the produced structures varying in elemental composition, shape, size, chemical and physical aspects.

2.2 Synthesis of vanadium nanostructures

(Chirayil et al., 1998) described easy way to prepare mesoporous rod-shaped nanostructures of vanadium based oxide through the hydrothermal process with V2O5 as vanadium pentaoxide major source and henylethylamine as reducing and structure Controlling Representative. The phase compositional and morphological characterizations of nanorods were achieved by X-ray diffraction (XRD) raiment of the synthesised sample was determined with a Philips PANalytical X'pert Pro diffractometer. Scanning electron microscopy (SEM) images were reserved by SEM (Hitachi S-4800), fortified with energy dispersive X-ray spectrometry (EDS). Morphology and size were looked into by TEM, the exact position and lattice parameters were Found from HRTEM and SAED. Transmission electron microscopy operated at a fast-tracking electric potential of 200 kilovolts. The nanorods are found up to few hundred nanometers in an extent, the size were 280–300 and 60nm. They verified that the key role is the molar ratio in productions of materials on the structure and the morphology aspects.

(Ding et al., 2009) synthesized V_2O_5 nano fibres and three metal vanadate with diverse configurations (MnV_2O_6 nano sheets, $FeVO_4$ nano needles and Sn_2VO_6 nanoparticles) through a hydrothermal process. They characterized the samples by XRD, EDX, SEM and TEM. The X-ray diffraction scrutiny was accomplished using a Rigaku D/Max diffractometer with Cu Kα irradiation at λ= 0.15418nm. The transmission electron microscopy (TEM) image, SAED array and energy spectra followed by a Hitachi-900 electron microscope worked at 100KV. The SEM descriptions were got by a dual beam-235 fixated ion beam (FIB) system activated with a stepping up voltage of 10KV. Electrochemical investigations in lithium batteries indicate that amongst this metal vanadate Sn2VO6 nanoparticles show the maximum ability, more than 1700 mAh g-1, and Can retain respectable capacity maintenance. They also examined the magnetic properties of MnV_2O_6 Nano sheets and FeVO4 nanorods.

(Wang et al., 2010) synthesized Iron cotted vanadium–tin oxide nanoparticles through hydrolysis and precipitation process, iron-II acetate, vanadium-III and tin tetra-chloride are used as harbingers. The incurred sample was sorted by X-ray diffraction (XRD) to check phase purity. An electronic contact among vanadium, tin and iron atoms in the oxide assembly was sustained by intends of X-ray photoelectron spectroscopy (XPS). They discover that iron class into the vanadium–tin oxide controlled the crystallite size and oxidation positions of vanadium and iron in the superficial area. They examined compassion measurements on CO gas measuring device, this iron nobbled nanoparticles demonstration alteration of the greatest sensitivity in the direction of the subordinate temperature direction.

(Avansi et al., 2015) evaluates the dye adsorption and photocatalytic response of orthorhombic V_2O_5 of 1D nanostructures (nanowires and nanorods), produced by a hydrothermal technique. The synthesised models were regarded as by X-ray powder diffraction (XRD), SEM and transmission electron microscopy for superficial topography and morphology, for measuring size use zeta sizer, Fourier transforms infrared spectrometry (FTIR). The dye adsorption ability and photocatalytic stuff were mainly studied, under visible light by the elimination of the methylene blue dye. Moreover, because of band gap values 2.6 eV, the nanostructures could be showing higher photoactivity than commercial V_2O_5, under visible light.

2.3 Characterization of nanostructures

(Krystek et al., 2011) described that the recent developments in the field of nanotechnology require a detailed characterization of nanoparticles due to its convenience for both synthesis and product development, as well as for safety studies. Particle size, shape, surface charge, surface area, and disparity are some of the most important parameters determining Particle properties, also used in defining NPs.

(Hubert et al., 2011) says, the main goal of fundamental characterization is the clarification of 3-D array of the fragments in a-solid. In employment, the key aim of structural characterization is evaluating the measurements and positions of the unit cell There are several categorization techniques have been reported for the characterization of semiconductors, Some of the most generally used techniques are Scanning Electron Microscope (SEM), X-Ray Diffraction (XRD), Photoluminescence (PL) and, Fourier transform infrared spectroscopy (FTIR), Raman Spectroscopy. Mainly these approaches are used to take image of the superficial, and thus characterize the surface morphology and features.

(Mittal et al., 2013) Most applications of nanoparticles require these properties to be homogeneous. Several methods exist to characterize nanoparticles. Among these the most widely used are UV–visible spectrophotometry, scanning electron microscopy (SEM), EDX spectroscopy, X-ray diffraction (XRD), Fourier transforms infrared (FT-IR) spectroscopy, HRTEM and dynamic light Scattering (DLS).

2.4 Applications of nanostructures in environmental remediation

(Sánchez et al., 2011) investigate Nanotechnology shows a key protagonist in the improvement of Environmental remediation science and engineering. Itis appropriate both for in-situ and ex-situ treatment of Environmental pollution and clean-up with High efficiency. Remediation involving nanoscale materials (known as nanoremediation) has several advantages over the traditional methods ofremoving Environmental contaminants. For example, it may reduce the clean-up time and the costs for cleaning up and it might Even decrease the absorptions of some contaminants to proximate zero. In general, nanoparticles remove pollutants from the environment through adsorption, redox catalytic reactions, and/or photocatalytic reactions.

2.4.1 Removal of contaminants by adsorption

(Qu et al., 2013) described Adsorption is improving Phase for eliminating organic and inorganic pollutants in wastewater treatment. Nano adsorbents have superior adsorption efficiency compared to conventional adsorbents because they offer Significant improvement of the surface area, choosiness, and adsorption kinetics. For example, (Zhu et al., 2013) magnetic nanocomposites Canbe used for subtraction of heavy metals (As,Cr, Hg, Pd) from water, due to Recycling of the material, this Makes the method very cost effective.

2.4.2 Redox catalytic degradation of pollutants

(Zhao et al., 2011) reported that Nano scale metals and bimetals as such Cu, Fe, Zn, Fe/Ni, Pd, etc. are particular active in destroying different organic and inorganic pollutants commencing soil and water. The reactivity of these Nano metal particles is typically extraordinary. For instance, NZVI is capable of Evenself-explode once exposed to an air. NZVI is one of the most extensively studied and commonly used nanoparticles for a treatment of a wide range of Environmental pollutants. (Chen et al., 2012) carried the effective elimination of the antibiotic metronidazole (MNZ) from aquatic solutions by NZVI particles. Moreover, NZVI can be used-as a very cost-effective means for the removal of antibiotics including amoxicillin (AMX) and ampicillin (AMP) from aqueous media.

2.5 Photocatalytic degradation of contaminants

(Bokare et al., 2008) investigate the removal of Orange G toxic organic dye, in aqueous suspension by means of Fe/Ni bimetallic nanoparticles. An analysis on degradation of lindane 120(gamma- hexachlorocyclohexane) by nanoscale Fe/Pd particles in aqueous solution revealed that Fe/Pd bimetallic nanoparticles completely dechlorinate 5 mg/L of lindane contained by 5min at a catalyst filling of 0.5 g/L via first-order kinetics. Photocatalytic degradation of contaminants, (H. H. Mohamed et al., 2012) reported that there are two General categories of Photocatalysis processes, catalyzed photoreaction and sensitized photoreaction, the first photo excitation happens continuously on the catalystthanphoto-excited catalyst transmissions an electron into a ground state molecule. In case of a sensitized photo excitation, the early photo excitation happens in engage able molecule (dye molecules), where they Relateto the ground state catalyst.

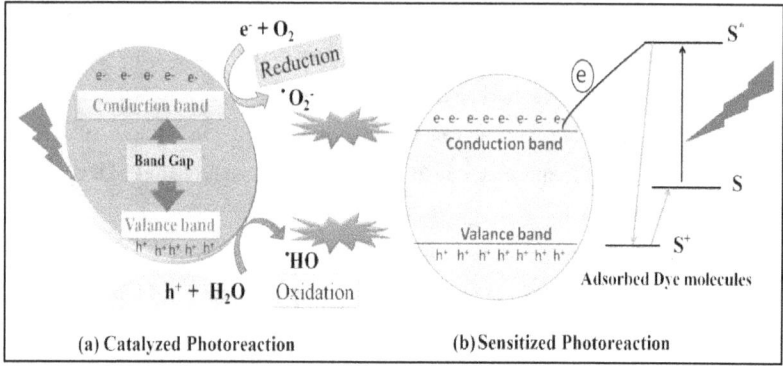

Figure 2.1: Schematic presentation of photocatalytic processes (Mohamed and Bahnemann, 2012).

(Qu et al., 2013) stated, Photocatalysis is proven to have huge ability due to low price, Environment-friendly and supportable water degradation technology. Particularly, the use of nanoparticles in this treatment technology is a very pertinent issue. Nanosized semiconductors such as nano-TiO2, ZnO, CdS, and WO3 are among the frequently used photocatalytic nanoparticles in wastewater treatment. In particular, TiO2 is the most preferred one due to low poisonousness, a chemical strength, a low price tag, and enormous availability as a material. However, the practical application of photocatalyst such as TiO2 has suffered from several limitations; for example, the need for using aqueous suspensions confines its extensive pricticaluse because of issues regarding separation of the residue and Recycling of the photocatalyst. Photocatalyst optimization to develop to make use of the visible light of solar radiation is another problem. Fortunately, the latter problem can be solved by either doping metals or anion impurities into nano-TiO2, using dye sensitizers, or blend nano-TiO2 with narrow band-gap semiconductors to form hybrid nanoparticles or nanocomposites.

2.5.1 Basic principle of photocatalytic oxidation process

(Ahmed et al., 2011) described that Photocatalysis is Advanced oxidation process (AOP) for destroying organic pollutants in the continuation of semiconductor photocatalysis (e.g., TiO$_2$, FeO), light source, and an oxidizing mediator. When the semiconducting catalyst is illuminated by photon energy equal/more than the band-gap energy (ΔE), it stimulates electrons from the valence band to the conduction band. At the same time, it formed an electron vacancy, a hole (hv), in the valence band.

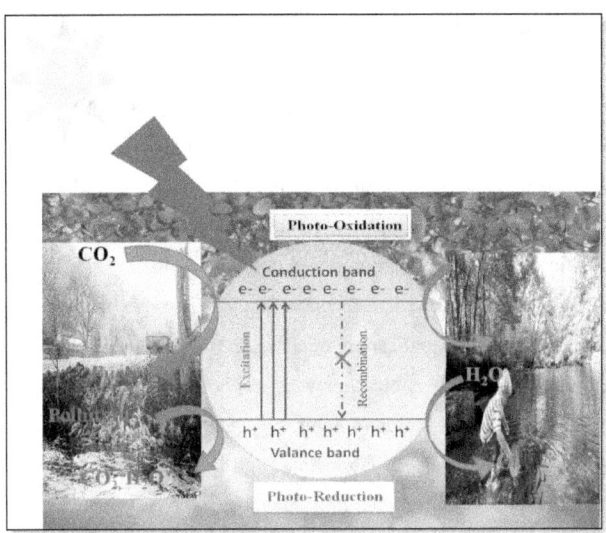

Figure 2.2: Graphic purposed diagrams illustrating the principle of photocatalysis.

(R. Mohamed et al., 2012) investigate the photogenerated positive holes oxidize with water to create hydroxyl radicals (OH•) meanwhile the electrons create superoxide radicals with reaction of oxygen. Both of these primary products, Specifically (OH•) are durable oxidizing sorts that outbreak organic contaminants.

(Ahmed et al., 2011) stated in the photocatalytic removal of carbon-based impurities, the degeneration fashion of oxygen and the oxidation of contaminants have to keep at the same rate. Otherwise, it will cause accumulation of electrons in the CB (usually if there is no Sufficient oxygen in the solution), thereby increasing the rate of the recombination of an ehp and delaying the photocatalytic oxidation process. Nevertheless, photocatalytic activities highly rely on the intrinsic properties of catalyst like crystal structure, surface extent, particle magnitude, band-gap and outward hydroxyl compactness of the photo catalysts.

2.6 Photocatalytic property of bismuth vanadate nanostractures

Metallic oxides (MO) semiconductors are generally considered for the photocatalytic applications due to high chemical exposure stability, easy to manufacture and inexpensive. Since, the TiO_2 was found to be a good photocatalyst for achieving photo-induced water splitting by Fujishima and Honda in 1972, several semiconductor photocatalysts are extensively investigated (Fujishima et al., 1972; Kudo et al., 1999; Madhusudan et al., 2012; Nagaveni et al., 2004; Sun et al., 2013; Wu et al., 1999). It is fact; TiO_2 calm down continues foremost economical photocatalyst representing the degradation of the many carbon-based compounds in UV light irradiation, but, TiO_2 is not so good associated with solar photocatalysis because of its wide band gap (~3.3eV), that limits the valid application of TiO_2 in sunlight (Linsebigler et al., 1995)so, the development of newly visible light assisted photocatalysts get into considerable attention owing to the visible radiation (400nm < λ < 800nm) which makes a great contribution to the solar spectrum. Thus, to fabricate a high level effective and efficient semiconductor photocatalyst is the current central issues in photocatalysis research (Joung et al., 2006; Tang et al., 2012; Wu et al., 2013; Yamasita et al., 2004; Zhang et al., 2013; Z. Zhang et al., 2010).

The photocatalytic response of $BiVO_4$ has been very much examined. The overall list of publications that have published on $BiVO_4$ as photocatalyst from 2012-2018 is presented in Figure 2.3. A sum up of 209 research studies on the photocatalysis activity of $BiVO_4$ has been published successfully in the last 6 years. It's noticeable that publications about $BiVO_4$ photocatalyst response undoubtedly represent a progressive trend, pointing out that $BiVO_4$ photocatalyst has comprised attractive interest in photocatalysis discipline.

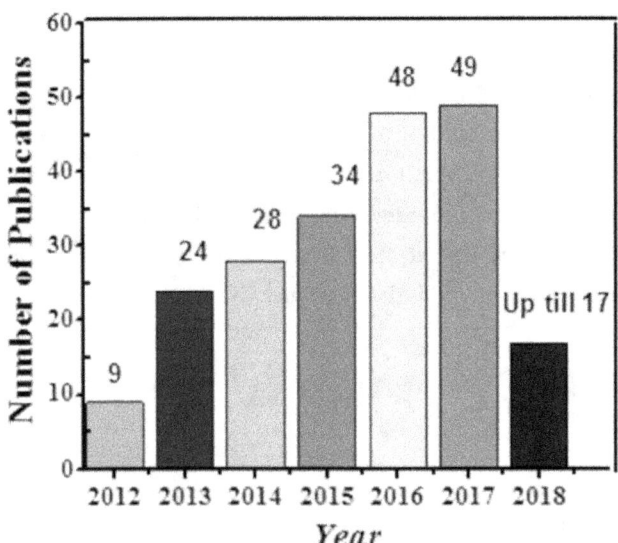

Figure 2.3: Number of scientific papers published on BiVO$_4$ based as photocatalyst from the last six years (source: http://www.scopus.com, search conditions: "BiVO$_4$" and "photocatalysis").

Bismuth vanadate (BiVO$_4$) is a new visible light dependent photocatalyst, it holds up to three primary crystalline phases, scheelite, monoclinic scheelite and tetragonal Zircon structures. Among them, monoclinic BiVO$_4$ (m-BiVO$_4$) with a band-gap of 2.4eV possessed peculiar light absorption properties. The m-BiVO$_4$ (2.4eV) exhibits superior photocatalytic efficiency when compared to tetragonal BiVO$_4$ (t-BiVO$_4$) with (3.1eV) because photocatalytic characteristics of BiVO$_4$ are strongly depended on crystal form. So, it's actually significant to look into the crystal structure of BiVO$_4$ in an easy method systematic to manufacture an effective crystalized visible light photocatalyst (Gotić et al., 2005; Guo et al., 2010; Hu et al., 2011; Ke et al., 2008; Zhang et al., 2011; Zhang et al., 2007).

In the beginning stage of BiVO$_4$ synthesis for photocatalyst activity, nanostructures were prepared through solid state reaction reactions in bulky particle size and small surface area. Several studies described the preparation and characterization of different nanosized BiVO$_4$ semiconductors photocatalyst by different methods. Here we have discussed literature survey according to the preparation methods.

2.6.1 Microemulsion (MEs) method

T. P. Hoar and J. H. Shulman were the first who used the term microemulsion in 1943. Since1980, colloidal structures which comprise microemulsion have comprised extensively looked into, particularly as the synthesis of nanomaterials for multifarious applications(Boutonnet et al., 1982; Hoar et al., 1943). The general representation diagram of MEs method is shown in figure 2.4.

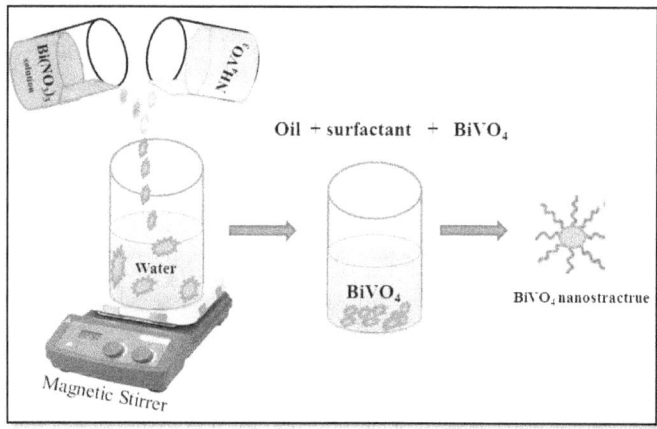

Figure 2.4: Schematic illustration of microemulsion method for the preparation of nanostructure.

(Ahmed et al.) used the MEs method to prepare bismuth Vanadate (BiVO$_4$) with good photocatalytic activity. The microemulsion method is a profitable route for synthesis substructures at comparatively modest temperature, the developed nanoscale powder exhibit higher uniformity in topography and small particle range as compared to other powders synthesis routes. The low and decreased particle size may be from nano range micelles that manipulated the particles maturation. Since grain and crystal sizes of BiVO$_4$ have highly dependent on synthesis temperatures. (Peng et al., 2008) synthesized m- BiVO$_4$ rods with micro size ~30-50nm, the m-BiVO$_4$ micro-rods photocatalyst having band gap ~2.31eV, give good photocatalytic response owed to high absorption efficiency and mixing of valance band O 2p and Bi 6s. The methylene blue dye nearly decomposed in one hour in solar light irradiation. (Liu et al., 2010) described three dimensions monoclinic bismuth vanadate with ordered macroporous by modified emulsifier-free emulsion polymerization approach. The synthesized material showed the excellent photocatalytic response in visible light illumination, the economic response of 3D-ordered microspores (3D-OM) of m-BiVO$_4$ flows from the superiority of possessing large surface area and higher surface oxygen vacancy concentration. (Chung et al., 2010) also reported BiVO$_4$ nanoparticles (Nps) with high purity and crystallinity they calcinationated the nanoproduct at 400, 500, 600 and 700°C, these Nps with particle size about 35nm, show enhance photocatalytic response under visible light illumination as compared to nanoparticles prepared by solid-state reaction (SSR) method, figure 2.5 shows the XRD pattern, while figure 2.6illustrates the SEM micrograph of these as-prepared BiVO$_4$ by MEs and SSR method.

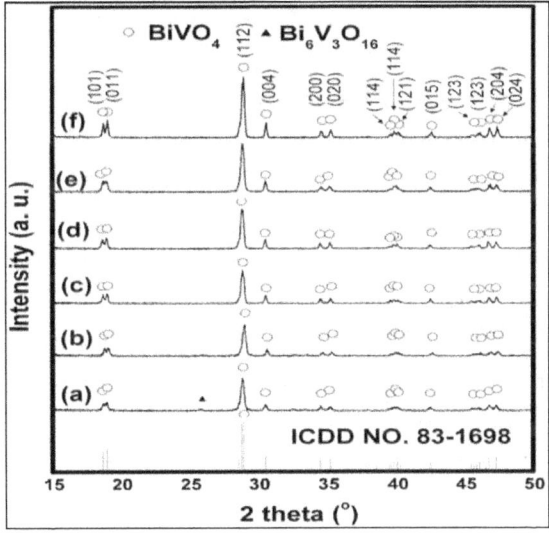

Figure 2.5: The XRD spectrum of microemulsion prepared powder at different temperature (a) 400°C for 10 min, (b) 400°C, (c) 500°C, (d) 600°C and (e) 700°C for 20 min and the solid-state derived BiVO$_4$ powders heated at (f) 700°C for 5 h.

Figure 2.6: SEM images of BiVO$_4$ nanoparticles prepared at (a) 400, (b) 500, (c) 600 and (d) 700°C for 20 min BiVO$_4$ powders and (e) BiVO$_4$ at 700°C for 5 h prepared by SSR.

2.6.2 Flame spray synthesis method

The first modern-era reactors for nanostructures flame spray (FS) synthesis route started out in the 1940s, become most effective in 1971, G.D. FS routes allocate the formulations of homogeneous nano-oxides with variable constitutions and different crystallized forms due to heats and higher quenching effects (Trommer et al., 2015). (Chatchai et al., 2009) synthesized amorphous and monoclinic BiVO$_4$ spherical nanoparticles using FS approach, these nanoparticles have asurface area was ~10-75 m^{2}g^{-1}. Since high crystallinity and surface are fundamental parameters to the photocatalytic activity of BiVO$_4$ although observing the pH of the solutions, in some cases heat treatment was also given for high crystallinity. (Dunkle et al., 2009) reported, the synthesized of BiVO$_4$ from ultrasonic spray pyrolysis, the structure of BiVO$_4$ was shaped by the dehydration, decay of diluter and precursor material, respectively. These BiVO$_4$ nanoparticles show the superior photocatalytic response for oxygen evolution in the visible illumination as compared to commercial BiVO$_4$ due to particle morphology difference. (Strobel et al., 2008) reported the flame spray synthesis of BiVO$_4$ yellowish powders pigment and added capsulize in SiO_2 to prevent thermal sintering and considerably to suppress photocatalytic activity. The schematic process of flame spray method is shown in figure 2.7.

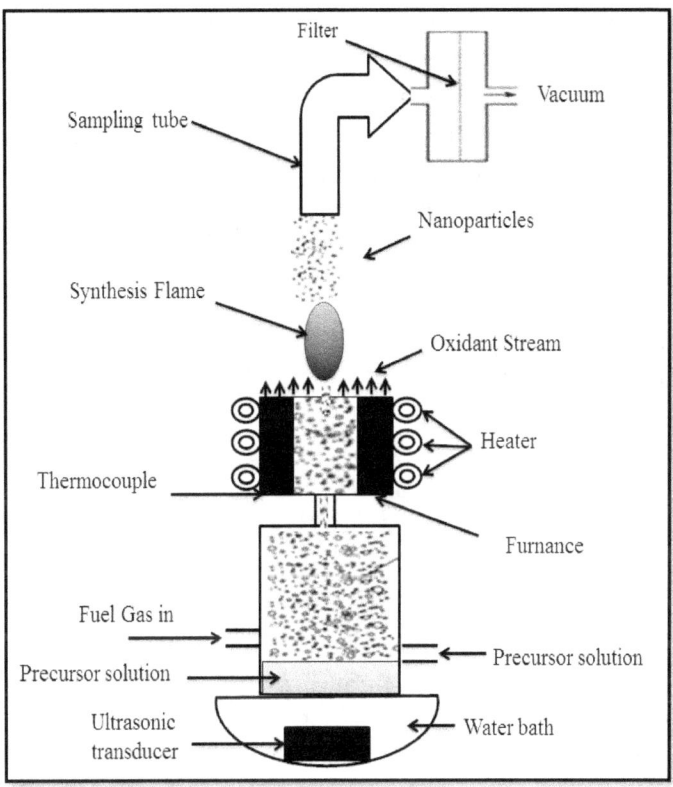

Figure 2.7: Purposed diagram of Flame spray method for the preparation of micro/nanostructure of $BiVO_4$ photocatalyst.

2.6.3 Ultrasonic-assisted method

The initiative Ultrasonic-assisted synthesis technique commenced in the 1940s, but became common in 1974 and the sonochemical process has received much consideration in materials preparation (Yin et al., 2009). In Ultrasonic-assisted method cavitation bubbles are created in the solution through ultrasonic waves, this action accomplished at comparatively high temperature ~5000°C and pressures of just about 500 atm that makes the constitution of smaller and uniform nanoparticles with great crystallinity than that of conventional techniques. The schematic diagram of ultrasonic-assisted method is showed in figure 2.8.

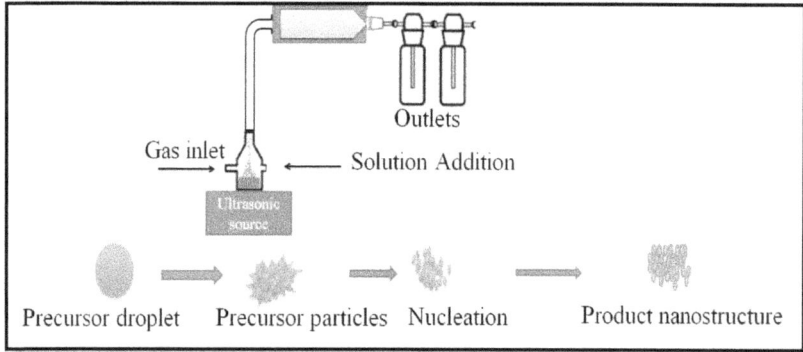

Figure 2.8: Schematic graphic diagram of ultrasonic-assisted method for the preparation of $BiVO_4$ based product nanostructures.

(Shang, Wang, Zhou, et al., 2009) synthesized nanosized $BiVO_4$ by ultrasonic assisted method, polyethylene glycol (PEG) was used as assistance. Ultrasonic irradiation treatment and polyethylene glycol influenced the structure of $BiVO_4$; the nanoparticles were of size 60nm. The photocatalytic activity for degrading organic dye in visible-light improved nearly 12-times as compared to previous reported $BiVO_4$ results prepared by solid state method. The photocatalytic competence of $BiVO_4$ improved owing to crystal size, band gap and as well as specific surface area. (Liu et al., 2010) investigated the preparation of particles are endorsed through form transformation path attained by ultrasound radiation, these m-$BiVO_4$ spindle grains exhibits higher absorption in the 400 $\leq \lambda \leq 800$ light spectra, and these spindle particles have superior photocatalytic efficiency as compared to $BiVO_4$ prepared by formal solid-state reaction to degradation of Rh-B in

$400 \leq \lambda \leq 800$ light radiation, which principally stimulated by the low crystal size and several crystal planes.

2.6.4 Microwave method

In 1971, the first time utilization of Micro Wave (MW) heating in chemical research has been reported, yet became most realized in 1986, this actuated various publications in this refreshing and novel approach, particularly in organic and suspension-stage chemical reaction (Bykov et al., 2001; Lidström et al., 2001; Whittaker et al., 1994). (Zhang et al., 2007) described MW-assisted aqueous process to getting stage controlled monoclinic $BiVO_4$ and tetragonal $BiVO_4$ nanopowders. The characterizations of the $BiVO_4$ powders were evaluated by X-ray diffraction (XRD), UV-vis spectrometer, TEM, and Raman spectrometer. The photocatalytic activeness of the manufactured $BiVO_4$ monoclinic and tetragonal powders was checked at sample organic toxic Rhodamine -B dye. They proposed that the photocatalytic response of m-$BiVO_4$ is much higher than t-$BiVO_4$ in a visible light spectrum, owed to an internal structure, small band gap, and the 6s2 lone pair of Bi^{3+}. (Yan et al., 2013) described the preparation of reduced graphene oxide bismuth vanadate composite from the MW-assisted process. They evaluated the photocatalytic activity of these GO-$BiVO_4$ composite for degrading of ciprofloxacin (CIP). The graphene oxide-$BiVO_4$ efficiency is 3 times higher than the pure $BiVO_4$ material. (Shi et al., 2013) reported the microwave-assisted method for the synthesis of $BiVO_4$ for the deprivation of ciprofloxacin (CIP) in visible illumination. (J. Li et al., 2014) synthesised m-$BiVO_4$ and CuO-$BiVO_4$ heterogeneous by microwave and impregnation-calcination method. The photocatalytic responseindicates that CuO loading efficaciously raises the photocatalytic actions of the materials which were checked from the decolouring of methyl orange (MO) toxic dye in visible light illumination. The p-n junction of CuO-$BiVO_4$ mixed nanocomposite raises the light absorption potential of semiconductor catalyst and interval of the activated charge carriers. (Moscow et al., 2016) synthesized floral shaped m-$BiVO_4$ from a facile microwave oven assisted method. This floral shaped m-$BiVO_4$ showed high photo-absorption properties under visible light with an energy band gap of ca. 2.3ev. The photocatalytic response was calculated by the decomposing of a toxic dye methylene blue and phenol by using H_2O_2 as an initiator in visible light irradiation. The floral shaped m-$BiVO_4$ holds up stability for the photocatalytic response even at fifth runs. The better photocatalytic activity for methylene blue, phenol degradation and photoelectron chemical response of m-BiVO$_4$ referred to the high crystallinity, optical dimension, and morphology. The schematic process is shown in figure 2.9.

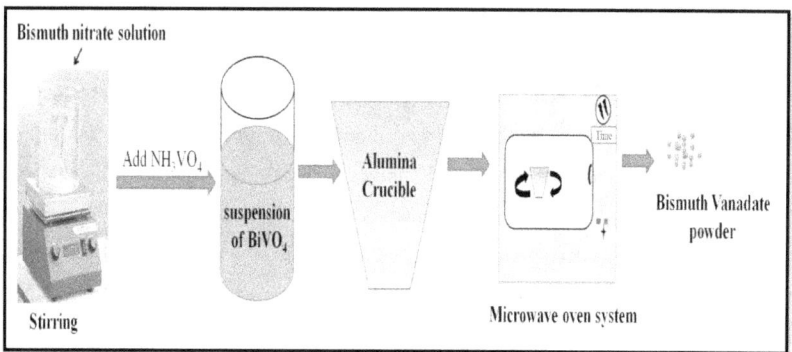

Figure 2.9: Schematic process of Microwave-assisted method for the preparation of BiVO$_4$ micro/nanostructures.

2.6.5 Coprecipitation method

Coprecipitation method is a chemical method which has many advantages, including low cost, simple way to control particle and crystal size, free from contamination and huge scale manufacture (Martinez-de La Cruz et al., 2010). (Ke et al.) described that they initial prepared, the amorphous BiVO$_4$ and subsequently a structure between tetragonal scheelite and monoclinic made up after heating at various ramp rate temperature. They observed that crystallinity and area had a higher effect on the photocatalyticresponse to decolouring MB dye. (Ke et al., 2008) developed m-BiVO$_4$ particles and reported that crystalized size and defects in crystallinity of nanoparticles had significant constituents and extremely affect the photocatalytic response. These defects are produced on the evaluation of oxygen and volatilization of bismuth vanadate as the calcination temperature comprised some 400°C, owing to these defects the recombination action came about to capture the photogenerated electron and hole pair that limiting the photocatalytic activeness. (Wang et al., 2018) prepared Bi$_2$FeVMoO$_{10}$ nanoparticles by cations substitutions in monoclinic BiVO$_4$ through co-precipitation method. The photocatalytic activity was checked by degrading Rhodamine-B dye solution.

Bi$_2$FeVMoO$_{10}$ nanoparticles reflect superior photocatalytic activity than BiVO$_4$ and α-Bi$_2$Mo$_3$O$_{12}$. The good photocatalytic activity is due to higher vacancies, large separation in the C$_B$ and V$_B$ and because of Fe^{3+}/Fe^{2+} redox couples. The schematic process of co-precipitation method is as illustrated in figure 2.10.

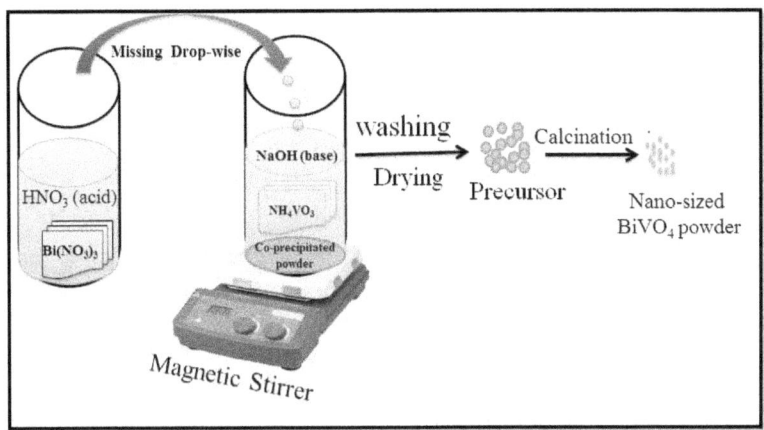

Figure 2.10: Schematic demonstration of coprecipitation method for the preparation BiVO$_4$ based nanostructures.

2.6.6 Sol-gel method

(Liu et al., 2005) synthesized m-BiVO$_4$ powder from a Photoassisted sol-gel method, it suggests 1.3 to 3 times superior efficiency than that of BiVO$_4$ synthesised through a conventional sol-gel method for the oxygen evolution reaction. The higher efficiency by the as-prepared BiVO$_4$ comprised because of either owing to tiny extent of BiVO$_4$ atoms or due to content activeness of the superficial part comprising Bi^{5+} and OH$^-$. (Wang et al., 2013) prepared m-BiVO$_4$ photocatalysts by the sol-gel method, they evaluated the influence of different pH amount on microstructure and photocatalytic properties. They calculated when pH value changes the morphology and photocatalytic response of the sample changes. They found that at low pH value the samples are irregular but with the increase of pH values the samples indicate granular structure mean aggregation. To valuation the photocatalytic responce of the as synthesised materials the methyl orange dye was degraded. In this case, the sample of pH value nine showed the narrow bandgap and reflects superior photocatalytic response. The process of sol-gel is schematically illustrated as in figure 2.11.

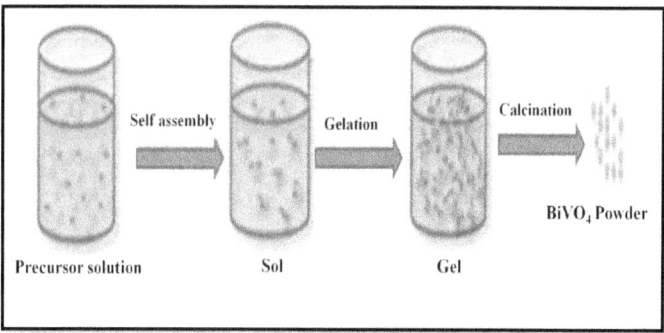

Figure 2.11: Schematic illustration of sol-gel process for the fabrication of BiVO$_4$ nanostructures.

2.6.7 Hydrothermal method

Hydrothermal synthesis in supercritical water back-number reputed easy, favorable and applicable process for the production of metal, oxide and multi-metal oxides compounds and has many advantages like a simple process, controllable particle size and gives high purity in addition to as intersections with great crystallinity. The grain size by metal oxide normally depends upon the hydrolysis order and soluble capability of the ingredients, for accomplish to ascertain of the solution on nucleation and crystallization by atoms, hydrothermal considerations of temperature and squeeze may comprise multifaceted in the water system. At present, there are a lot of studies about the fabrication of BiVO$_4$ nano photocatalyst by hydrothermal method (Xi et al., 2010). (G. Wang et al., 2012) prepared BiVO$_4$ and CoPi /BiVO$_4$ by hydrothermal method, found cobalt phosphate BiVO$_4$ greatly enhanced photocatalytic response, these exhibited that effectual electro-catalyst of H$_2$O oxidization may comprise as well a good catalyst as O$_2$ development by photocatalytic H$_2$O oxidation. (Hu et al., 2018) synthesized by facile hydrothermally and sol-gel method BiVO$_4$/TiO$_2$ for photocatalytic degradation of Benzene currently known as among the most harmful contaminants, under visible light. (Hu et al., 2016) stated the hydrothermal preparation of m-BiVO$_4$ photocatalyst and evaluated the influence of degradation in visible light decomposition of aqueous paracetamol has inquired by four different m-BiVO₄ semiconductor catalytic agent in the visible light, these catalytic agents with varied morphology followed to put down aqueous paracetamol contamination. Cube-like BiVO₄ powders showed higher photocatalytic responce. The excellent Photocatalytic response can be owed to the slow electron holes recombination in the catalyst. Figure 2.12; shows the schematic process of hydrothermal synthesis process.

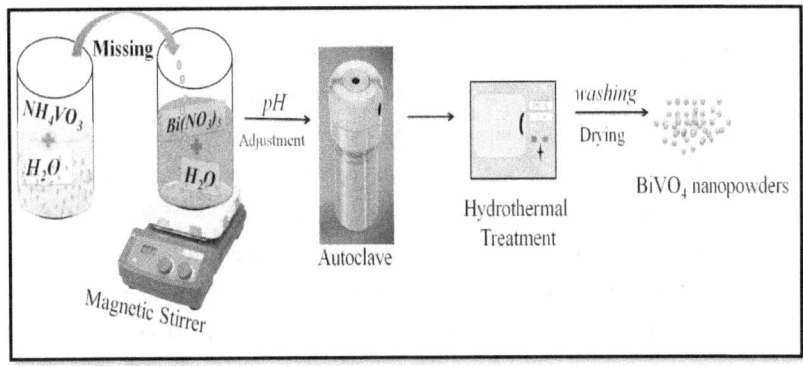

Figure 2.12: Schematic illustrations for the synthesis of BiVO₄ via hydrothermal method.

2.6.7.1 Hydrothermal method without any additives

(Zhang et al., 2007) reported that they synthesised tetragonal and monoclinic mixture of BiVO₄ powders at room temperature by aqueous processes, after, as prepared BiVO₄ were calcinated at temperature ~140°C to 200°C only m-BiVO₄ remained, this m-BiVO₄ demonstrated greater photocatalytic efficiency as to degrade the methylene blue suspension under visible illumination (420 ≤ λ ≤ 800) as compared to t-BiVO₄, it revealed that crystalline phase have very important effect on the photocatalytic response from BiVO₄. (Wang et al., 2009) reported that the morphology has also had great influence on the photocatalytic action. They synthesized bismuth vanadate nanoribbons of uniform shape, hundreds of microns the length 60-80nm wide and thickness stylish range 15-20nm. The as-synthesized nanoribbons showed higher photocatalytic activenesses in the abasement of eosin Y in visible light radiation. This may comprise credited to unique topography due to the great expanse of area. (Ren et al., 2009) described, synthesis of monoclinic bismuth vanadate nanotube, it delivered hexangular baffle parts with length 1.2 micrometer, breadth two hundred nanometer and thicknesses of 30 nanometers. The photocatalytic response of m-BiVO$_4$ nanotube was much higher as compared to bulk BiVO$_4$; it might be attributed owing to the special tubular structure. (Ahmed et al., 2018) synthesized surfactant free m-BiVO$_4$ nanoribbons by easy solvothermal route for photocatalytic degradation of organic toxic dye. The prepared photocatalyst exhibited effective photocatalytic activities up to 97% in 30 min for the decomposition of methylene blue dye in visible radiation illumination. The developed photocatalyst constitutes reusable and exhibited very micro commute inactiveness after three succeeding cycles. This more superior action attributed to higher surface area and purity, which intend the auspicious application of m-BiVO$_4$ nano-ribbons as a novel and highly economical photocatalyst for the degradation of organic pollutants. (Xu et al., 2014) synthesized m-BiVO$_4$ nano and microstructures with different morphologies nanoplates, dendrite leaves-like, sub-micro rods, and micro flowers by a template-free hydrothermal method. They claimed that pH and solution value has a great influence on the formation of crystal structures. The photocatalytic efficiency of the samples were checked by decomposing of methylene blue toxic dye in visible light illumination; showed good photocatalytic responce can be attributed of unique morphology and excellent ehp separation.

2.6.7.2 Hydrothermal method using surfactants

Generally, small crystal sizes and large surface are considered excellent for their photocatalytic applications referable great adsorption/desorption values of constituent contaminants, but most of them as above synthesizes BiVO$_4$ method produces great crystallization sizes and small surface area which are not appropriate for photocatalytic response so, these disadvantages were swept over by introducing surfactant in the hydrothermal synthesis method. The surfactant has a significant effect on the structure, such as to adjust morphology, crystal form, crystallinity and surface area of the product. Hence, BiVO$_4$ photocatalysts are developed in the comportment of different surfactants at various considerations and concentrations. (Ke et al., 2009) prepared the m- BiVO$_4$ via cetyl trimethyl ammonium bromide (CTAB) as a surfactant, at 200°C by hydrothermal method. CTAB alienated the topography of BiVO$_4$ and transfer the impure crystal phase to pure crystal monoclinic stage. The m-BiVO$_4$ showed the higher photocatalytic response for O_2 evolution in visible radiation illumination than that of amorphous $BiVO_4$ phase due to saturated monoclinic crystal form. (Zhang et al., 2006) synthesized m-$BiVO_4$ nanosheets of thickness 10-40nm by sodium dodecyl benzene sulfonate (SDS) as surfactant. The nanosheets showed higher photocatalytic efficiency as compared to bulk $BiVO_4$ under visible irradiation for the decolonization of Rhodamine. (T. Yang et al., 2009) reported that $BiVO_4$ spheric and decahedral were synthesised through varying the response temperature in front of the template, sodium-dodecyl-sulphate. The SDS highly influenced the photocatalytic response of bismuth vanadate to evaluate O_2 under visible light irradiation. (Li et al., 2009) too described the preparation of square plate resembling type, cuboid resembling type and flower resemble like bismuth vanadate through varying the pH and CTAB values. The photocatalytic response was practically improved as compared to degradation of methyl orange in solar radiation. Other aspects, such as phase purity and topography likewise too impacted the photocatalytic efficiency of $BiVO_4$. (Wang, 2017) reported a facile method for the preparation undoped $BiVO_4$ film, using the facileseed-assisted hydrothermal method. The $BiVO_4$ showed highest photo electrochemical than that of previous reported values. They investigate that the amount of polyvinylpyrrolidone (PVP) plays a vital role to tune the crystal, and causes of electron-hole separations. The photocatalysis significantly affected by the morphology, crystal size, phase and crystallinity. The additive of surfactant greatly influences the crystal structures and phase which directed to various photocatalytic activities. (Yin et al., 2009) claimed that m-$BiVO_4$ synthesized via CTAB-assisted aqueous hydrothermal method had greatly effective photocatalyst decolouring of Rhodamine-B in visible light as compared to $BiVO_4$ synthesized through aqueous method and by SS reaction.

2.6.7.3 Hydrothermal method using other additives

To control crystal phase, crystallinity and morphology the alternative way is additives of other organic and inorganic that is adaptable as same as the surfactants. (Sun et al., 2009) reported $BiVO_4$ nanoplates-stacked star-like synthesis using the chelating agent as ethylenediamine tetra acetic acid (EDTA), It has noticed that morphology of $BiVO_4$ so much dependent upon the molar concentration of EDTA to Bi^{3+}. The product showed much higher Photocatalytic action response than the previous reported $BiVO_4$ along solid state reaction approach subordinate visible light to degrade the methylene blue. (Ma et al., 2009) synthesized $BiVO_4$ microspheres, the result indicates that malic acid acted as central characters in morphology dominance of $BiVO_4$. It showed good photocatalytic under visible light radiation for the degradation of RhB. (Zhou et al., 2010) synthesized $BiVO_4$ particles that have great crystallinity and same morphology by applying K_2SO_4 as accumulative, which directed $BiVO_4$ to superior photocatalytic response for O_2 evolution.

2.6.8 Modification of $BiVO_4$ photocatalyst with Novel-metal, metal and Non-metal element

Up to now, the photocatalyst efficiency of pure bismuth Vanadate ($BiVO_4$) represents yet low due to its insufficient adsorption properties and Fast recombination value from the photoassisted created ehp charges. Alternation in the $BiVO_4$ put up increment the photocatalyst response, specified as the entry of noble metallic element assemblage, co-catalysts and metal doping for speed up the separation of ehp and to efficacious enhance the area of visible radiation use.

2.6.8.1 Noble metal deposition

Fermi levels are more low-level in noble metals than the $BIVO_4$ photocatalyst, the initiated electron as of the conduction band to the noble metallic element stuck at the surface of the photocatalyst, hole in valance band persist on the photocatalysts, so the chance of charges recombination brought down that leads in enhance photocatalytic response (A. Zhang et al., 2010a) Noble metal deposition on $BiVO_4$ also influence crystal structure, morphology and absorption of light that effect photocatalytic activity (Kohtani et al., 2005). (Ge, 2008b) made up monoclinic $Pd/BiVO_4$ and $Pt/BiVO_4$ composite through impregnation process and their photocatalytic activity was checked, the doping greatly enhances the photocatalytic efficiency of $BiVO_4$ in visible-light illumination to degrading of methyl orange. (A. Zhang et al., 2009) investigated the Ag-doped $BiVO_4$ composites, the results show that the efficiency of these $Ag/BiVO_4$ composite showed higher photocatalysts response equated pure $BiVO_4$, it might be attributed to high electron-hole separation. (Ge, 2008a) synthesized $Pt/BiVO_4$ composite photocatalyst by the impregnation method. The Photocatalytic activeness of the $Pt/BiVO_4$ composite comprised by measured the methyl orange degrading in visible light ray. The effects show that the photocatalytic response is clearly enhanced after the Pt was loaded.

(Merupo et al., 2016) synthesized Ag-doped m-BiVO$_4$ nanoparticles through high energy ball milling technique. The as-synthesized samples were with a spherical form of 50-100 nm. Ag doping significantly increased the photocatalytic efficiency for the degradation of acid blue organic dyes. The Ag-doped BiVO$_4$ nanocomposites exhibit efficient visible light dependent photocatalytic action attributable to charge dispersion at the semiconducting-metal interfaces and the participation of a radiation increased by Plasmon resonance effects at the surfaces of Ag-clusters.

2.6.8.2 Metal doping

Transitional metallic doping and the rare-earth element doping to BiVO$_4$ modify the charge carrier separation in visible light illumination (Xu et al., 2011). (Yao et al., 2008) inquire that the photocatalytic response from BiVO$_4$ as H$_2$O oxidization, found extremely increased from molybdenum doping, this enhancement from the photocatalytic efficiency by molybdenum doped BiVO$_4$ comprised due to the changes of the surface acidity of the photocatalyst. (A. Zhang et al., 2010b) prepared Eu-doping monoclinic BiVO$_4$ photocatalyst; it shows good photocatalytic activity in visible light illumination may be due to electron-hole separation. Eu/BiVO$_4$ showed red shift as compared to the pure BiVO$_4$ catalyst. (B. Liu et al., 2018) synthesized BiVO$_4$/SiO$_2$/reduced graphene oxide via hydrothermal method. The photocatalysis activity was checked against the degradation of the C.I. Reactive Blue 19 under the visible light radiation. The entry of RGO (reduced graphene oxide) demonstrated the high dispensability of photocatalyst in solution and the superior absorbance of positive metallic ions that increased its photocatalytic activity.

2.6.8.3 Non-metal doping

Numerous study is reported in literature about the nonmetallic doping, (Lee et al., 2010) prepared C loaded BiVO$_4$ (C-BiVO$_4$) composite throughan impregnation method. The C-BiVO$_4$ complexes demonstrated higher photocatalytic efficiency than that of BiVO$_4$. The degradation efficiency for RhB organic dye visible radiation (400 $\leq \lambda >$ 800 nm), it was noticed that 3 wt% carbon-BiVO$_4$ demonstrated the most high-level Photoassisted catalytic efficiency about 95% in 180 min. The high efficiency by carbon BiVO$_4$ comprised due to the large surface area, high adsorption capability and separation between electron-hole pairs. (Zhang & Zhang, 2010a) fabricated silicon metalloid doping into BiVO$_4$, they used metallic organic decomposition reaction method for synthesis, the as-prepared Si-doped BiVO$_4$ film displayed effective photocatalytic activeness in the visible radiation. It may be owed due to the modification in crystal size, surface expanse, optic surface assimilation and charge separation. (Shang, Wang, Sun, et al., 2009) synthesized spindle-like BiVO$_4$ nanoparticles by polyaniline and by sonochemical access. They claimed that sonochemical prepared nanocomposite possess sharper efficient photocatalytic effect for the decay of tetraethylated Rhodamine in visible radiation at (800 ≥ λ > 400nm). This superior photocatalytic response may comprise due to synergic consequence of PANI/BiVO$_4$, which stimulates the detachment of charge carriers. (Appavu et al., 2018) reported the synthesis of novel nitrogen-doped RGO/BiVO$_4$ by the hydrothermal method the photocatalysis test were checked for the degradation of methylene blue, congo red and anti-biotic metronidazole and chloramphenicol under visible light. Photocatalytic responce was enhanced owing to the concentration of N-rGO in BiVO$_4$. Similarly, the HPLC analyses showed that dyes and antibiotics were both decomposed to the maximum level. (Ahmed et al., 2017) reported the preparation of carbon fibrecoted m-BiVO$_4$ microspheres by hydrothermal method against the photocatalytic decomposition of methylene blue (MB). They observed that the immobilization of m-BiVO$_4$ photocatalyst at the surface of carbon fibres has not reduced the visible light absorption capability as compared to pure m-BiVO$_4$. Carbon fibercoated m-BiVO$_4$ showed an enhanced reusability. This higher activity and reusability of the photocatalyst may attribute due to the higher extent immobilization of photocatalyst.

2.7 Preparation of film

In the above discussion, we get BiVO$_4$ photocatalyst in powder form. In powder form there is a need of filtering process which is required to eliminate photocatalyst from the suspension which is tedious and expensive. So, the immobilization of BiVO$_4$ at the substrate is becoming a versatile fashion and popular due to the elimination of filter process of BiVO$_4$ from the suspension. BiVO$_4$ films with good photocatalytic efficiency are reported, prepared by various routes (Sayama et al., 2006). (Xie et al., 2010) prepared m-BiVO$_4$ film using citrate-precursor chemical process indicted of nanoparticles of 100nm size. The decomposition activity of acid orange comprised 78.9 % in 3h and essentially continued steadily in ten continual cycles in visible-light irradiation (400≤λ

≤800nm). (Zhang et al., 2008) prepared $BiVO_4$-MCM-41 hetro junction photo-assisted catalyst via substrate m-$BiVO_4$ on the MCM-41 molecular. The BiVO4-MCM-41 composite has greater surface areas that improve its photocatalytic response for decomposition of methylene blue dye, might be owe to the increment of adsorption operation. (Lamm et al., 2017) reported bismuth vanadate ($BiVO_4$) thin films of 50, 100, 200 and 300 nm thickness. $BiVO_4$ prepared via spray pyrolysis on glass coated with FTO, the $BiVO_4$ thin film showed enhanced efficiency as photo-anode material. It was suggested that due surface related limitation and inherent bulk, strategies such as doping or co-catalysis necessary for $BiVO_4$ to produce high O_2 production. They claim that combination of illumination with alkaline alters the chemistry of $BiVO_4$ surface for high oxygen evolution reaction. (Su et al., 2016) reported $BiVO_4$/Zn:$BiVO_4$ thin film prepared by spin-coating on FTO substrate, as fabricated $BiVO_4$/Zn:$BiVO_4$ displayed anticipating semiconductor for photoelectrochemical (PEC) water splitting in the visible light. Zinc doping handling turned down the Fermi level from the outermost region of $BiVO_4$ and made a $BiVO_4$/Zn: BiVO4 composite on the internal part of $BiVO_4$. The charge carry-over process over the depletion domain of the $BiVO_4$ electrode comprised of increased and the surface trappings of photogenerated electrons was invalidated, which directed to a raised PEC execution. (Lamm et al., 2017) reported the fabrication of uniform deposition of thin film m-$BiVO_4$ by Atomic Layer Deposition technique on FTO substrate, for the solar water splitting. The as-synthesized $BiVO_4$ by ALD enables for future development independent of substrate properties. $BiVO_4$ with better control over stoichiometry permits for the development of effective multi-layer appliances with advanced architectures. (Ullah et al., 2018) synthesized m-$BiVO_4$ and Se-doped $BiVO_4$ thin films for photocatalyst owing to high stability, narrow bandgap as well as facile for preparation. The Se-doped $BiVO_4$ showed ~38 to ~50 kcal/mol adsorption energy as compared to $BiVO_4$ for Photocatalytic water splitting. (Venkatesan et al., 2018) prepared stable monoclinic $BiVO_4$ thin films which were nontoxic and with narrow band gap ~2.4eV which permits the direct photo-assisted activation in visible light. Photocatalytic activity was investigated for Rhodamine 6G toxic dye.

2.8 Other synthesis method

(Li et al., 2008) discovered the formulation of mesopores monoclinic $BiVO_4$ photocatalyst through solution combustion method with silica as surface surfactant, as-prepared $BiVO_4$ made superior photocatalytic activity compared to commercialized $BiVO_4$, for the decomposing of methylene blue (MB) organic dye and oxidization of nitrogen-oxide (NO) gas in the visible radiation. The schematic diagram of BiVO4 preparation by silica template is shown in figure 2.13.

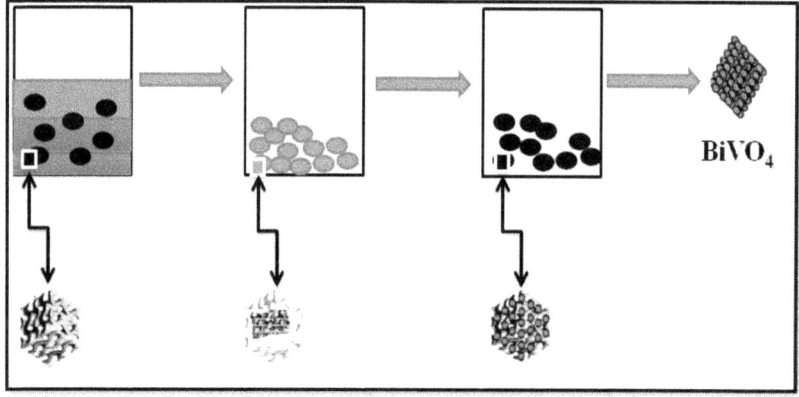

Figure 2.13: Schematic diagram of silica template assisted method.

(W. Li et al., 2016) reported the synthesized of $BiVO_4$ microspheres photocatalyst with different crystalline phases by simple thermal treatment methods. The photocatalytic efficiencies of the materials were checked through the decomposition of organic standard dye methylene blue (MB) under the visible irradiation. They observed $BiVO_4$ sample prepared at 400°C, that was of mixed crystalline forms tetragonal and monoclinic $BiVO_4$ give the best effective potential for the degradation. (Nguyen et al., 2017) prepared tetragonal m-$BiVO_4$ hetero-structure by solvothermal method, applying the various molar ratio of EGME/H_2O solvents. The photocatalytic response of these materials was deliberated for the decomposition of RhB in visible light irradiance. The obtained $BiVO_4$ photocatalyst showed the good response for decomposition of Rhodamine B in visible light.

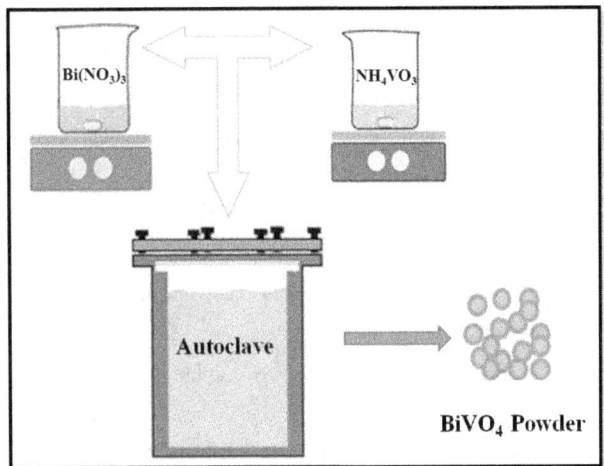

Figure 2.14: Purposed diagram for the fabrication of BiVO$_4$ nanoproduct by solvothermal method.

2.9 Znic vanadate nanostructures

(Melghit et al., 1999)Investigated a new method for the preparation of Zinc pyrovanadate at room temperature, they use zinc oxide powder and vanadium oxide as starting agent, this method consists of two steps, first is the preparation of zinc oxide from a zinc chloride solution ZnCl$_2$. The second step consists of dissolving a vanadium oxide xerogel V$_2$O$_5$·2H$_2$O, prepared by an ion exchange method, in distilled water. The pH of the solution, which stabilized around 5.6, was almost constant. Zinc pyrovanadate was prepared according to equation given below.

$$V_2O_5 \cdot 2H_2O \text{ (aq)} + 3 \text{ ZnO} \cdot 0.3H_2O \text{ (s)} \rightarrow Zn_3(OH)_2V_2O_7 \cdot 2H_2O$$

They characterized the samples by XRD patterns for structural measurement were performed on a D/Max-IIIA diffractometer via Cu Kα radiation with λ=1.54056 Å, at a scanning rate of 0.07° s^{-1} for 2θ ranging from 5° to 90°. DSL curve was used to check the thermal characteristics. They also predicted that by using the same solution, it has been possible to prepare new metastable phases of indium and chromium vanadate.

(Luo et al., 2015) synthesized 1-D zinc vanadate based nano fibers by electro spinning under an annealing process. This method is simple and efficient, these nano fibers are promising high performance. They used Zinc acetate dehydrate

($C_4H_6O_4Zn.2H_2O$), Poly vinyl pyrrolidone (PVP), N-Dimethylformamide (DMF) and isopropyl alcohol. They characterized the samples by X-ray diffraction (XRD), energy dispersion X-ray fluorescence analysis (EDAX), Raman scattering were done for chemical composition and for structure of nano-ribbons. The morphology and structure were checked by TEM, SAED and HRTEM.

(LZ Pei et al., 2015) synthesized Zinc vanadate ($Zn_2V_2O_7$) nanorods via a simple and facile hydrothermal approach. The zinc vanadate nanorods were characterized by XRD, SEM, TEM, FTIR. And Uv-visible They claimed that Sodium dodecyl sulfonate (SDS) has an crucial role in the materialization of $Zn_2V_2O_7$ nanorods. The photocatalytic activity of the zinc vanadate nanorods checked through the photocatalytic deprivation of methylene blue organic dye in the solar light. They suggested that the $Zn_2V_2O_7$ nanorods show favorable potential for the photocatalytic decomposition of organic contaminants in the solar light irradiation owing to structure, morphology, size pH, hydrothermal temperature, duration time and SDS concentration.

2.10 Ferric vanadate nanostractures

Ferric vanadate ($FeVO_4$) has been widely utilized for a photocatalyst dye treatment under visible radiation. The advantages of the compound admit a narrow band gap for visible radiation immersion, extensive availableness, low-priced and fine stability. It's well known that the photocatalytic activity of the materials greatly connected to their structures and morphology. $FeVO_4$ has four diverse polymorphs called as $FeVO_4$-I, $FeVO_4$-II, $FeVO_4$-III, and $FeVO_4$-IV, from which $FeVO_4$-I represents a stable form constituted at room temperature as others are metastable phase that are normally conceived at high pressure and eminent temperature. In $FeVO_4$-I, Fe_3^+ ions bear three crystallographic places from which two locates are deformed octahedral FeO_6 and one locate is in distorted trigonalbipyramidal FeO_5 surround. Fe-O polyhedra build 6 columns doubly damaged chain and the chains are brought together by VO_4 tetrahedra to build 3-D frames. Still, the low photocatalytic activity by pure $FeVO_4$ gives limited it's encourage apply in practical applications owed to it has low adsorptive execution and migration difficulty of photo-generated electron-hole pairs. To overcome these problems, several efforts have made up induced to raise the activity of $FeVO_4$ based photocatalysts.

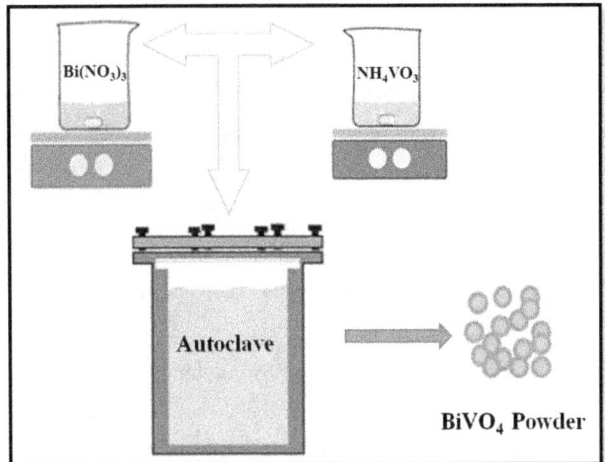

(Hu et al., 2013) synthesised Ferric vanadate (FeVO$_4$) nanoparticles as visible light photocatalysts through microwave irradiation method. They evaluated the physical and chemical aspects by applying X-ray diffraction and scanning electron microscope. The photocatalytic responce of the as synthesised samples were observed by studying the decomposition of the MB organic toxic dye in the visible light irradiation. They reported different parameters like, solution pH values as well as the amount of H$_2$O$_2$ and catalyst amount, heat treatment temperature of FeVO$_4$ effect the photocatalytic degradation of MB. Their results showed at pH value within the range of 1.5-2.0, excellent photodegradation 99 % under visible-light illumination within 40 minutes was gained.

CHAPTER 3

MATERIALS AND METHOD

The materials and chemicals that were used during the synthesis process are given below in table 3.1.

Table 3.1: shows the various materials and chemicals, the detailed of the suppliers are also provided for references.

Materials / chemicals	Formula	Purity	Supplier
Ammonium metavanadate	NH_4VO_3	99.6%	ACROS, Belgium, USA.
Vanadium pentaoxide	V_2O_5	99.4%	Merck, Darmstadt, Germany.
zinc acetate	$Zn(O_2CCH_3)_2$	99%	Merck, Darmstadt, Germany.
Ferric chloride	$FeCl_3$	99%	Aladdin Chemistry Corp. China.
Bismuth nitrate	$Bi(NO_3)_2$	99%,	ACROS organics, Belgium
oxalic acid	$C_2H_2O_4$	99.4%	ALDRICH
Sodium hydrate	$NaOH$	99%	Merck, Darmstadt, Germany
Deionized water	H_2O	99%	ALDRICH
Ammonia solution	HNO_3	99%	Aladdin Chemistry Corp China.
Poly-vinyl-pyrrolidone	PVP	99%	ACROS, Belgium, USA.
Cetyltrimethylammonium bromide	CTAB	99%	ALDRICH
Ascorbic Acid	$C_6H_8O_6$	99%	ALDRICH

All chemicals were analytic grade reagents and used without further purification. This research was consisted of two steps, first one was about the preparation, and characterization of the chemically active materials, the second parts of this research was involved for the application of these materials as photocatalysis and Bio-sensor related application. The experimental route is schematically showed in fig below.

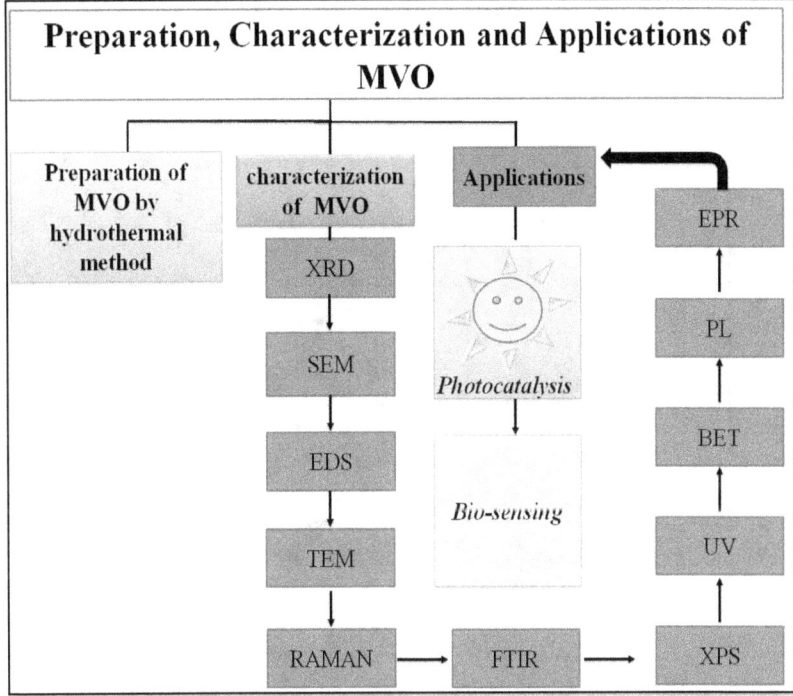

Figure 3.1: Schematic flow chart of preparation, characterization and application of MVO.

3.1 Hydrothermal method

Hydrothermal process is a method to synthesis pure single crystals. These crystals are developed in hot water under high pressure, this pressure depends upon the solubility of the precursors, the synthesis is performed in an apparatus that is named autoclaved, that is Teflon lined with different sizes, in the Teflon, the solution is poured that containing precursors for crystalline material growth along with water. A temperature gradient is maintained at opposite side of the growth autoclave so that the hotter end dissolves the precursors and the cooler end facilitates the growth of crystal seeds. The Flow chart of the hydrothermal method is Illustrated as in figure below.

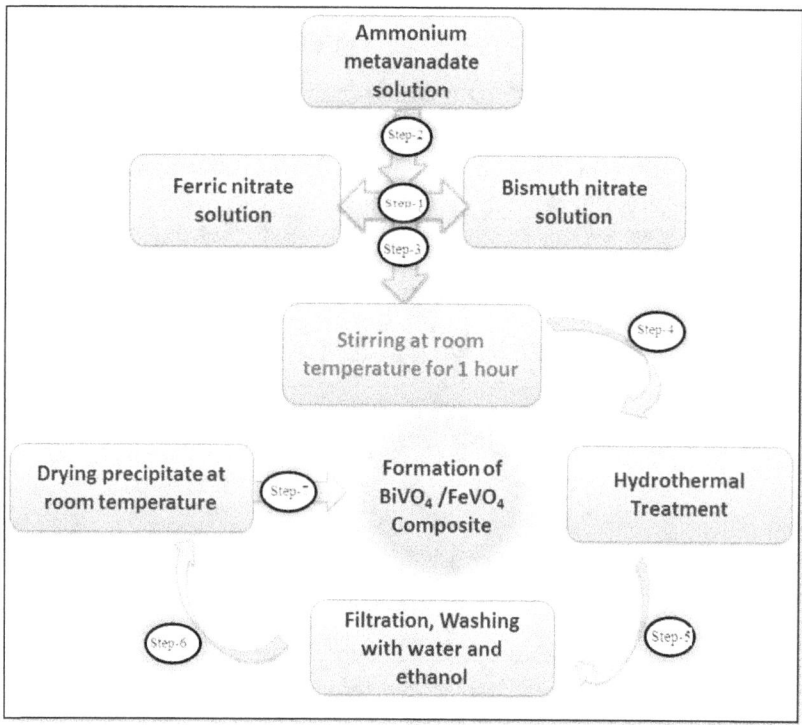

Figure 3.2: Flow chart of the hydrothermal method for the fabrication of MVO.

The development of ingredients with high vapor pressure closely to their melting point can be suitably performed. This technique is correspondingly appropriate for the development of huge, good superiority crystals, in spite of the fact that maintain respectable control over their compositions. The disadvantage comprises the essential need of costly autoclave and impossibility of seeing and observing the crystals as this one matures. The stainless steel autoclave of different sizes, which is used for the preparation of MVO is shown in figure 3.3 below.

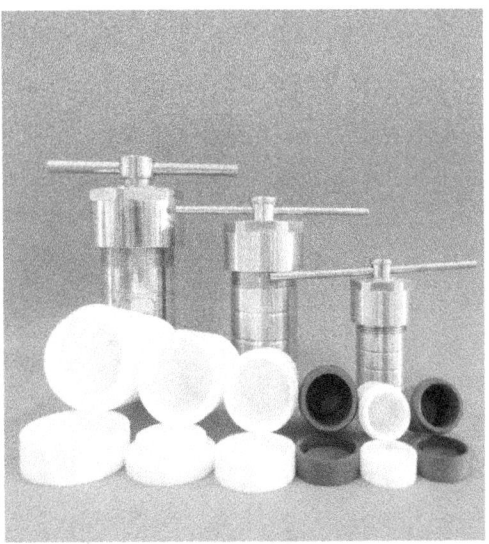

Figure 3.3: The Stainless steel autoclave used for the synthesis of MVO during the hydrothermal method.

3.2 Photocatalysis

To check photocatalytic responses of powdered MVO, samples were illuminated under Xenon lamp of an accumulative intensity of 300 W to degrade different organic dyes in visible-light irradiation, the distance involving the reactor and the lamp was kept 25-30 cm. For the kinetics, dyes solutions with fixed concentrations (150 ml) were prepared and appropriate amount (50, 100, 150mg) of the as-synthesized MVO were mixed in each dye solution separately. The obtained solutions were stirred vigorously for 15 min in dark and illuminated under visible light. Before starting the experiment pH of the solutions was maintained according to required experimental conditions. The final solutions were centrifuged (10000 rpm for 5 min) and nitrogen cooling system HX-DC1006 was given throughout the experiment to avoid any thermal degradation and to keep the temperature at 0°C. The degradation of the dyes solutions was analyzed using Perkin Elmer, lambda 35 UV/Vis spectrometer in the spectral range of 400-800nm. The Schematic diagram for absorption spectra is showed in figure 3.4 below.

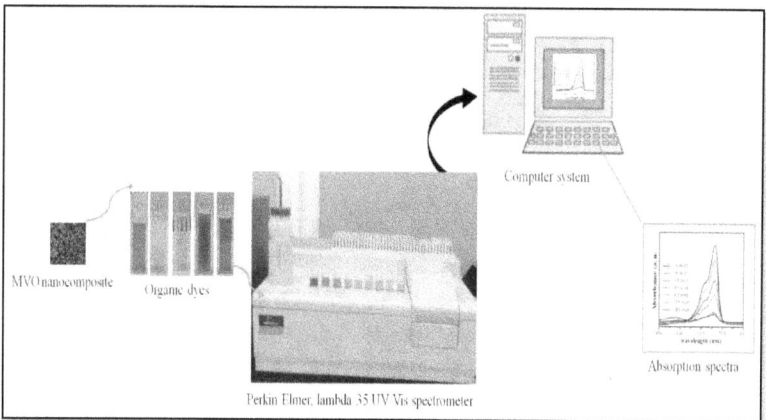

Figure 3.4: Purposed diagram for absorption spectra using Uv/visible spectrometer for different dyes.

3.3 Electrochemical sensing

The electrochemical evaluation was carried using a model CHI-760D electrochemical working station, and a three-electrode scheme; the apparatus which is used for electrochemical sensing of Bio-molecules are illustrated in figure below. Electrochemical Impedance spectroscopy is a versatile tool for analysis of conductivity, surface analysis, and electron transfer while Cyclic voltammetry is a common bio-sensing method of measuring the reduction potential of a species in solution. A cyclic voltammogram is a plot of current versus applied voltage. To begin the experiment, a potential is applied that is much more positive than the potential of the reference electrode.

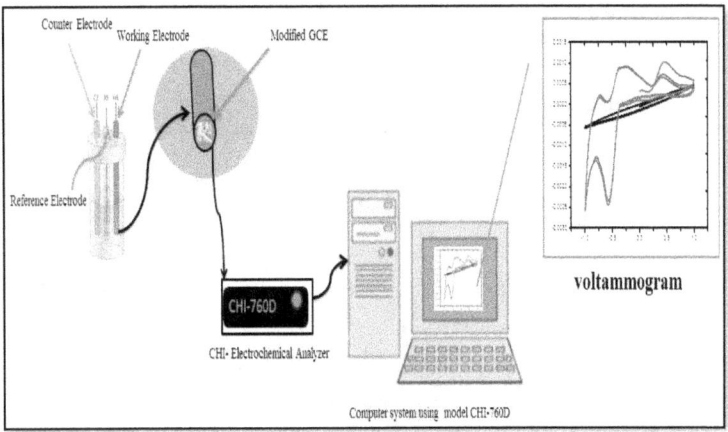

Figure 3.5: Purposed Schematic mechanism Electrochemical CHI-760 analyzer for the Bio-sensor application.

3.4 Experimental setup and working

The heterojunction composite MVO were fabricated via hydrothermal method; here we will discuss one by one preparation of these metal vanadates.

3.4.1. Synthesis of BiVO$_4$ nanostructures

In a typical synthesis, 2 mM [5 ml HNO$_3$ solution (5 M/L)] of (Bi(NO$_3$)$_3$.5H$_2$O)was gradually added to 1 mM (20 ml) of NH$_4$VO$_3$ dissolved in 5 mL of NaOH (5 M/L) solution. Upon addition, a homogenous suspension was formed which was stirred for 1 h to ensure complete homogenization. The pH was adjust around 8 of the system using 2.5 M/L ammonium hydroxide solution. Subjected to hydrothermal treatment in a Teflon lined stainless steel autoclave at 180°C for 24 h. After the completion of hydrothermal treatment, the resulting yellowish precipitates were collected and thoroughly washed with deionized water (D.I.W) and absolute ethanol to ensure removal of surface bound impurities. The product was dried at 80°C for 8 h before using it for the photocatalytic degradation of organic dyes.

Synthesis procedure suggested for the preparation of BiVO$_4$ nanoparticles illustrated in Fig. 3.6.

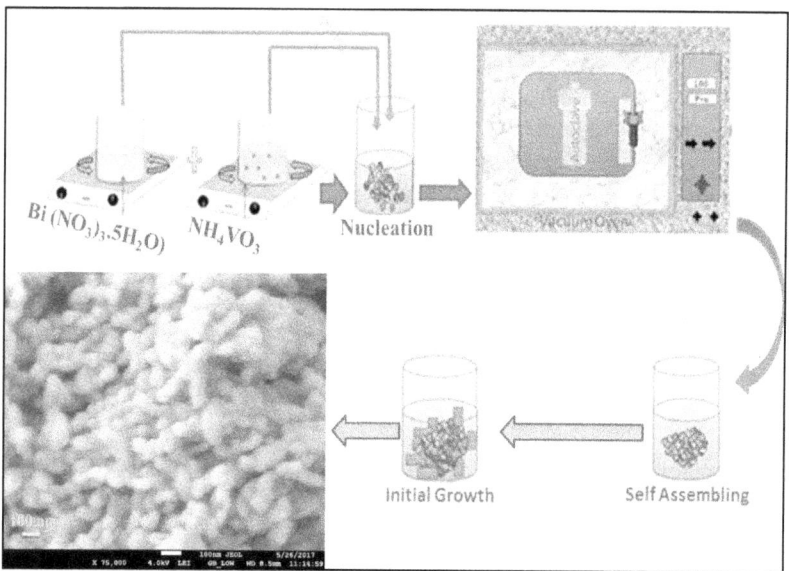

Figure 3.6: Schematic illustration for the hydrothermal growth of BiVO$_4$

3.4.2. Synthesis of FeVO$_4$ nanostructures

. For the synthesis of FeVO$_4$, the stoichiometric quantity of Fe (NO$_3$)$_3$.9H$_2$O, NH$_4$VO$_3$ (2.052g), NaOH and polyvinylpyrrolidone (PVP) was resolved in H$_2$O on an individual basis. The liquefied Fe (NO$_3$)$_3$.9H$_2$O was added together into Triton X-100 in 100 ml of distilled H$_2$O under vigorous stirrer and then NH4VO3 was added up, followed by sodium hydroxide solution. The pH of the solution was adjusted at about 8. The preceding solution was stirred for another one-half an hour and poured into autoclave for hydrothermal treatment and kept undisturbed for 24 hours at 180°C. The prevailed precipitant was water-washed various times with double distilled water and ethyl alcohol to get rid of impurities and then dried for 8 hours at 60°C. At last, the materials were calcined at 600°C for 3 hours.

Synthesis procedure suggested for the preparation of FeVO₄ nanoparticles illustrated in Fig. 3.7.

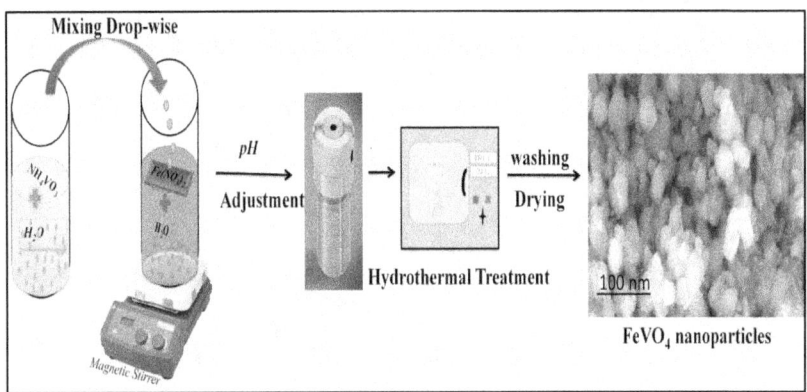

Figure 3.7: Purposed synthesis procedure for the preparation of FeVO₄ nanoparticles.

3.4.3. Synthesis of Zn₃(VO₄)₂ nanostructures

In a typical method, 1.4037 g of Ammonia Vanadate, 1.3170g of zinc acetate and 0.8163g of CTAB were dissolved in 40 mL N, N-dimethyl formamide (DMF), Oxalic acid ($C_2H_2O_4$) was added drops wise as a chelating agent respectively under vigorous stirring for 2 hr. Oxalic acid turns the solution colour into yellowish that suggests chelation from oxalate anions to metal cations. Sodium hydrate (NaOH) was used to adjust the pH of the solution. The change of colour from yellow to bluish indicating the reduction of V^{5+} into V^{4+} (Hoard et al., 1971; Llordes et al., 2011; Sathyanarayana et al., 1964; Tracey et al., 1987) It's far a recognized fact that (DMF) can absorb water from the precursor materials to produce $NH(CH_3)_2$ and HCOOH, this HCOOH further serves as reducing agent and result in a final product of $Zn_3(VO_4)_2$ with V^{3+}(Mao et al., 2008). The mixture was transferred to a 100 mL autoclave with a Teflon line. The autoclave used to maintain at 180°C for 20 hours after that the autoclave was cooled openly in the air. The white precipitates had been filtered, washed with deionized water and ethanol for many times and dried at 80°C for 8h.

Synthesis procedure suggested for the preparation of $Zn_3(VO_4)_2$ nanoparticles illustrated in Fig. 3.8.

Figure 3.8: Growth procedure for the synthesis of $Zn_3(VO_4)_2$ nanoplates.

3.4.4. Synthesis of BiVO₄/FeVO₄ composite

The heterojunction composite BiVO₄/FeVO₄ were fabricated via hydrothermal method, Firstly 1 mmol $Bi(NO_3)_3·5H_2O$ and 1 mmol $Fe(NO_3)_3·9H_2O$ were dissolved in 60 ml distilled water, then 2mmol of NH_4VO_3 were poured into it and vigorous stirring were carried out for 1 h at ambient temperature. The pH was adjusted through NaOH and HClsolution, the solution transferred into 100 ml

Teflon-lined stainless autoclave at 180°C for 24 h. After cooling the autoclave the precipitate was centrifuged and washed many time with ethanol and distilled water then dried at 80°C.

The flow chart of the preparation method is shown in figure 3.9 below.

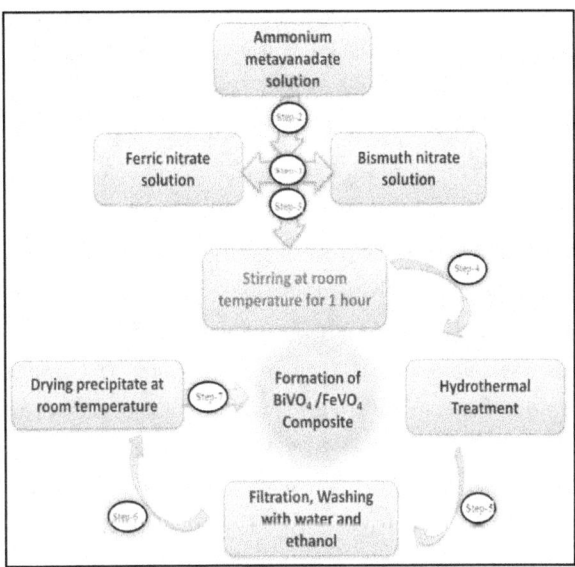

Figure 3.9: Flow chart of the hydrothermal method for the preparation of BiVO$_4$/FeVO$_4$.

3.4.5. Synthesis of Zn$_3$(VO$_4$)$_2$ /BiVO$_4$ composite

For the heterojunction composite Zn$_3$(VO$_4$)$_2$/BiVO$_4$ initially, 1 mmol of Bi(NO$_3$)$_3$·5H$_2$O and Zn(O$_2$CCH$_3$)$_2$ were dissolved in 100 ml of distilled water, yellowish Colour of solution is obtained on addition of 2mM NH$_4$VO$_3$, which was stirred for an hour. The HCl and NaOH solutions were used for pH adjustment. The solution was transferred into 100 mL Teflon-lined stainless autoclave and subjected to hydrothermal treatment at 200°C for 48 h. After completing the reaction the autoclave was cooled down naturally, the precipitate was collected and washed numerously with ethanol and distilled water to eliminate the surface-bound impurities then dried at 80°C overnight.

3.5 Structural Characterization Techniques of MVO nanocomposites

Structural characterizations of MVO include the determination of their morphology, size and crystallinity. In the present work structural characterization were done by X-ray diffraction (XRD) was executed on (XRD, X'Pert MPD) diffractometer using monochromatic Cu Ka ($\lambda=0.15418$nm) radiation with a scanning speed of 2θ min-1. The structure, morphology and size of the particles were examined in field emission scanning electron microscopy (FESEM, Hitachi-S5500) equipped with an energy dispersive X-ray spectroscopy (EDS). FT-IR by FT-IR Spectrometer – Nicolet iS50, ranges from 400 to 4000 cm-1. Raman analysis through, LabRAM HR Evolution (HORIBA Scientific), by using 532nm laser as excitation source at room temperature. The Brunauer-Emmett-Teller (BET) surface area of the products was analyzed by an N_2 adsorption-desorption isotherm curve observed at 77.55K in a Nova 3200e surface area analyzer micrometric system. A multipoint BET method was exploited to calculate the surface area. For photoluminescence (PL) the 325nm line of a He-Cd laser was utilized as the excitation source in at room temperature, using a Hitachi luminescence spectrometer (F-4500). Electronic Spin Resonance (ESR) analysis was checked on ESR-JES-FA 2010 spectrometer. UV-vis-NIR diffuse reflectance (DRS) measurements were executed on a UV/vis/NIR spectrometer (Perkin Elmer, Lambda-35).

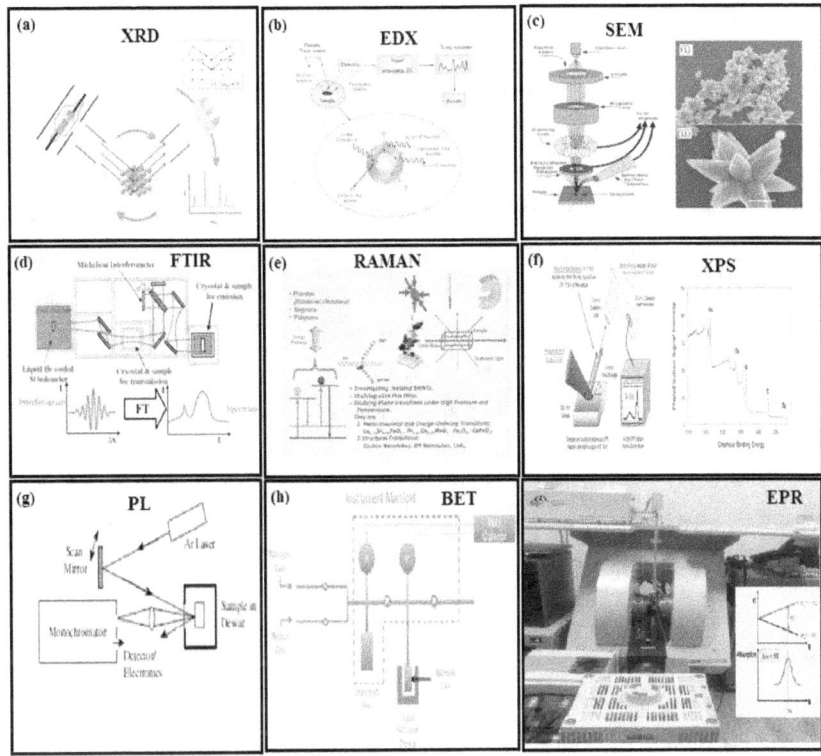

Figure 3.10: Nanomaterials characterization techniques. **(a)** X-ray diffraction (XRD), **(b)** Energy dispersive X-ray (EDX)spectroscopy, **(c)** Scanning electron microscopy (SEM), **(d)** Fourier transform infrared spectroscopy (FTIR), **(e)** Raman spectroscopy **(f)** X-ray photoelectron spectroscopy (XPS), **(g)** Photo luminance spectroscopy (PL), **(h)** Brunauer-Emmett-Teller (BET) surface area analyzer and **(i)** Electronic paramagnetic Resonance (ESR) spectroscopy.

CHAPTER 4

Section-I

RESULTS AND DISCUSSION

This chapter is dedicated to give the detail of preparation of $BiVO_4$, $FeVO_4$, $Zn_3(VO_4)_2$, $BiVO_4/FeVO_4$ and $Zn_3(VO_4)_2/BiVO_4$ hetrojunction nanocomposite for the photocatalysis and electrochemical sensing application, This chapter is divided into five sections, 1) Preparation of $BiVO_4$ nanostructure, 2) Preparation of $FeVO_4$ nanostructure, 3) $Zn_3(VO_4)_2$ nanostructure, 4) preparation of $BiVO_4/FeVO_4$ nanostructures and 5) $Zn_3(VO_4)_2/BiVO_4$ nanocomposite, by Hydrothermal method which were further used for photocatalytic and Bio-sensing applications respectively.

4.1 Hydrothermal Fabrication of monoclinic Bismuth Vanadate (m-$BiVO_4$) Nanoparticles for Photocatalytic Degradation of toxic Organic dyes

4.1.1 Introduction

In the present section we synthesized template free novel monoclinic Bismuth vanadate (m-$BiVO_4$) nanoparticles using facile hydrothermal method. The as-synthesized nanostructures were highly dispersive in nature with uniform size of 20-30nm. Bismuth vanadate nanoparticles exhibited efficient visible light photocatalytic degradation of organic toxic dyes (Rhodamine-B and Crystal violet). For phase, composition and chemical purity, the as-synthesized nanoparticles were characterized by using X-ray diffraction (XRD) and energy dispersive X-ray spectroscopy (EDX). To expose the morphology and topography, scanning electron microscopy (SEM) and transmission electron microscope (TEM) techniques were used. For the ascription of functional groups Fourier transform infrared spectroscopy (FTIR) was employed. The surface area of the as-synthesized nanoparticles was analyzed via Brunauer–Emmett–Teller (BET) and found to be 24.946m^2/g and pore diameter 1.932nm; m-$BiVO_4$ nanoparticles showed enhance photocatalytic response for the degradation for both dyes under visible light. PL study indicates the ability of the m-$BiVO_4$ nanoparticle for visible light devices.

4.1.2 X-rays diffraction (XRD)

Fig. 4.1.1 represents the XRD pattern of the hydrothermally synthesized bismuth vanadate at 180°C. XRD pattern corresponds to monoclinic scheelite structure of BiVO$_4$ having space group: I2/b, a = 5.193, b = 5.089, c = 11.697, γ = 90.387, well matched with the (JCPDS card No. 75-1866), that show good purity of material.

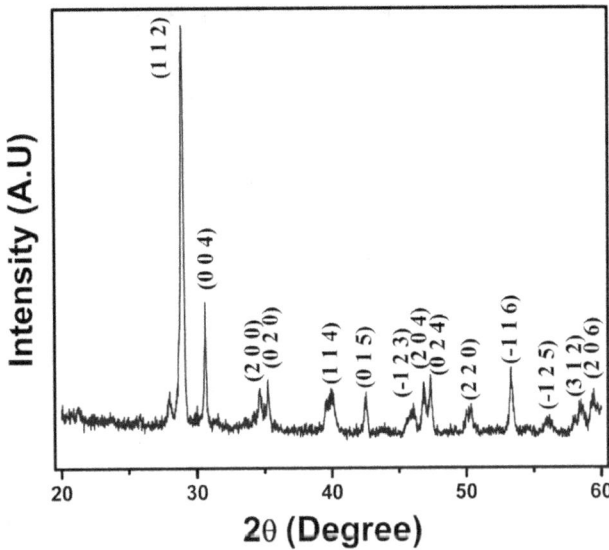

Figure 4.1.1: The XRD pattern for the as-synthesized BiVO$_4$ nanoparticles

Texture coefficient depicts the preferential or random growth of material. The texture coefficient for every hkl plane of BiVO$_4$ has been calculated from the X-rays diffraction (XRD) pattern by using following equation (Mikhailik et al., 2006).

$$Texture\ Coefficiet = \frac{I_{(hkl)}/I_{o(hkl)}}{\frac{1}{N}\Sigma_n(I_{(hkl)}/I_{o(hkl)})} \qquad (4.1)$$

Where,

$I_{(hkl)}$ = Intensity of particular XRD peak

$Io_{(hkl)}$ = Intensity of reference peak

N = Number of diffraction peaks consider in analysis

Texture coefficient (C_{hkl}) provides the information about preferred crystal growth direction. C_{hkl} value more than unity indicates the preferential growth direction for certain plane in a diffraction pattern. In our pattern, highest C_{hkl} value is 3.721998 for (-125) plane, the preferred growth orientation is associated to the maximum number of grains along (-125) plane, which can be considered as preferential growth orientation for the formation of nanoparticles as observed in the SEM and TEM images.

Table 4.1: X-ray diffraction intensities and preferred growth orientation factor for $BiVO_4$

HKL	I	Io	TChkl
(1 1 2)	810	100	0.029012
(0 0 4)	257	28.4	0.673629
(2 0 0)	129	18.0	0.533486
(0 2 0)	143	18.1	0.588117
(1 1 4)	120	6.9	1.294608
(0 1 5)	115	10.9	0.785376
(-1 2 3)	88	5.3	1.235984
(2 0 4)	129	21.5	0.44664
(0 2 4)	138	20.9	0.491517
(2 2 0)	97	9	0.802297
(-1 1 6)	166	13.4	0.922167
(-1 2 5)	70	1.4	3.721998
(3 1 2)	97	9.1	0.793481
(2 0 6)	125	8.4	1.107737

4.1.3 Scanning electron Microscopic (SEM) analysis

Fig. 4.1.2 shows the representative micrograph of $BiVO_4$ nanostructures obtained from scanning electron microscope (SEM) at high magnification. SEM images of as prepared materials revealed that nanoparticles were highly dispersed with uniform size of 20 to 30nm, which is also confirmed by TEM analysis (Fig. 4.1.2b). Sharp morphology indicates the feasibility of formed nanostructures for the photocatalytic application. SEM images at higher magnification endorse the development of nanoparticles. Small accumulations of nanoparticles were also noticed that may be due to inter-particle interface in the hydrothermal synthesis route. Fig. 4.1.2(c) represents the energy dispersive X-ray spectroscopic analysis, for chemical composition of the as-synthesized BiVO$_4$ indicating high crystalinity of the product. Only Bi, V, and O peaks were observed, while Cu and C peaks appear due to the holding grids (Meng et al., 2017).

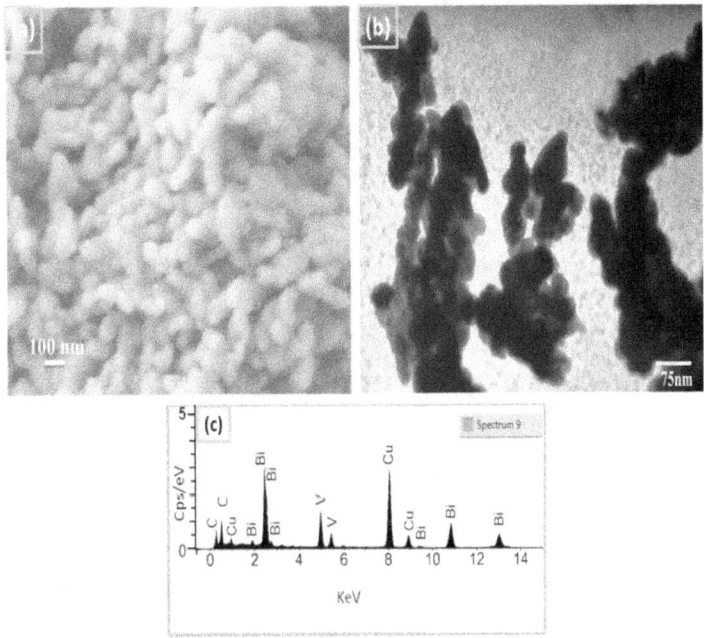

Figure 4.1.2: (a) SEM image at magnification (X75000) (b) TEM image of BiVO$_4$ nanoparticles (c) EDX pattern of BiVO$_4$ synthesized by hydrothermal method at 180 °C.

4.1.4 Fourier Infrared Spectroscopy (FTIR)

Fig. 4.1.3 shows the FT-IR spectrum of m-BiVO$_4$, confirming the presence of diverse functional groups related to BiVO$_4$. The spectrum shows the absorption peak at 706.73 cm^{-1} corresponding to VO$_4$. The band of V-O stretching is positioned at 519.12 cm^{-1}, the band at 948.38 cm^{-1} is allotted to weak absorption of the Bi-O bond (Niu et al., 2013). The symmetric and asymmetric stretching vibrations of V-O are further observed at 961.28cm^{-1}, 1004.94cm^{-1} and weak absorption at 477.70 cm-1 corresponding to Bi-O bond. The IR bands of very small intensities at 3586.76cm⁻¹, 3340.98cm⁻¹, 1634.85cm⁻¹ and 1137.82cm⁻¹ in the sample correspond to the traces of organic impurity adsorbed on the shallow of the synthesized sample using hydrothermal process (Yabuta et al., 2017).

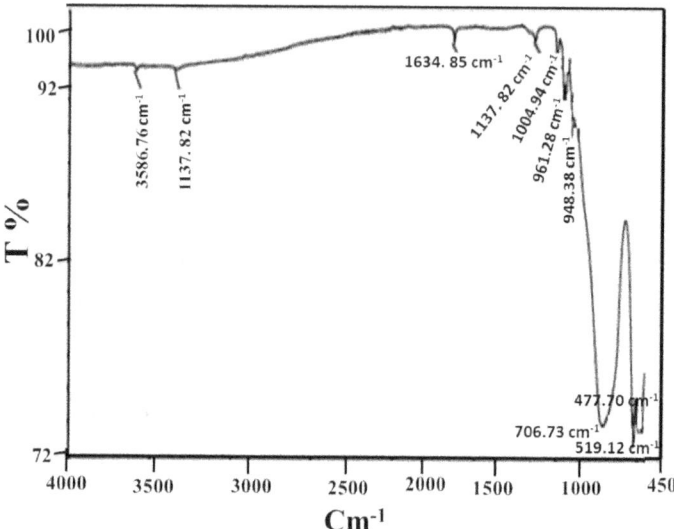

Figure 4.1.3: FT-IR spectrum of m-BiVO$_4$ synthesised by hydrothermal method at 180°C

4.1.5 Brunauer-Emmett-Teller (BET) surface area analysis

Fig. 4.1.4 indicates the nitrogen adsorption-desorption analysis by the Brunauer-Emmet-Teller (BET, ASAP-2020) to get the specific surface area of BiVO$_4$, the BET surface area of bismuth Vanadate is 24.946 m²/g. It is viewed that a stepwise adsorption and desorption hysteresis characterize by type-IV isotherm is retained, representing specific micro porous material because of pore condensation and pore diameter 1.932nm. The pore size Fig. 4.1.4 (inset) shows the distribution array from 1.4020nm to 32.1047nm.

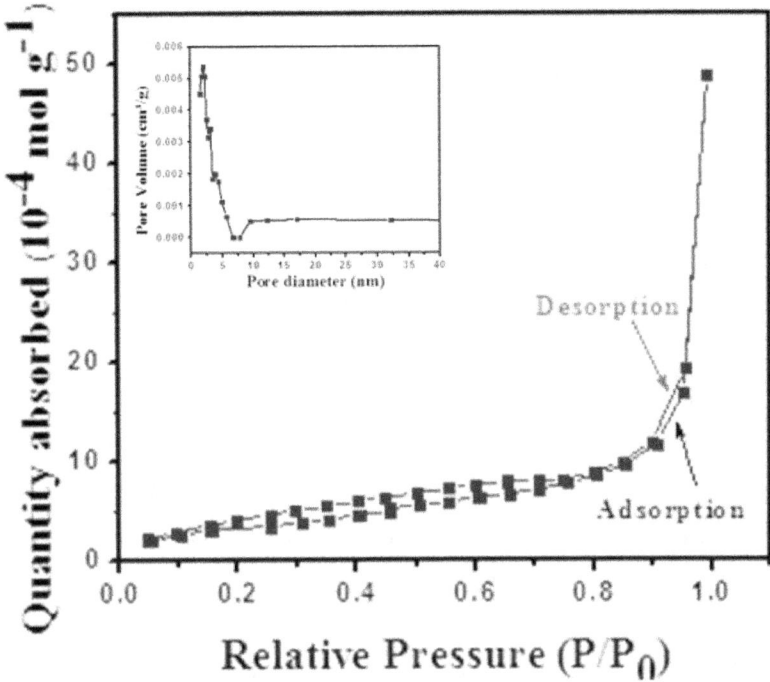

Figure 4.1.4: Nitrogen adsorption-desorption analysis of m-BiVO$_4$ and pore diameter (inset) by Brunauer-Emmet-Teller.

4.1.6 Photocatalytic activity

The catalytic activity of hydrothermally prepared m-BiVO$_4$ nanoparticles is shown in Fig. 4.1.5 (a, b). Tauc's plot method is used to analyze the optical band gap as depict in Fig. 4.1.5(a) (inset) (Brack et al., 2015; Jo et al., 2015; Sivakumar et al., 2015), The band gap energy for the direct transition is 2.42 eV for m-BiVO$_4$ nanoparticles which is consistent with previous reports (Jo et al., 2015; Thalluri et al., 2013; Xiao et al., 2017). The effect of photocatalyst on photo-degradation rates of RhB and CV was analyzed at different time intervals. The final solutions were examined using Perkin Elmer λ 35 series spectrophotometer indicating the maximum adsorption peaks at 553nm and 583nm for RhB & CV organic dyes, respectively. The efficiency of photocatalytic degradation was measured using following equation:

Degradation Efficiency (%) = $(C_0 - C)/C_0 \times 100$ (4.2)

Where, C and C_0 represent the specific and initial dyes concentration for the given time interval respectively.

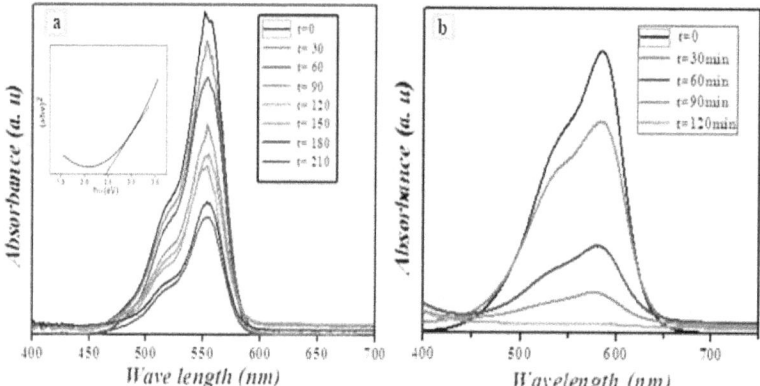

Figure 4.1.5: (a) Photocatalytic degradation of Rhodamine-B (RhB), in inset UV-visible badgap calculated by Tauc plot method (b) Photocatalytic degradation of Crystal Violet (CV)

After increasing the reaction time, visible photo-degradation rate of the organic dyes is found to decrease as shown is Fig. 4.1.5(a-b). The photocatalytic degradation efficiency is 96.23% of organic dye CV for 2 h and 84.81% of RhB dye for 3.5 h respectively. To elaborate the reaction kinetics Pseudo first order equation was employed;

$$\ln(C/C_0) = -Kt \quad (4.3)$$

Where C represents the concentration at specific time, C_0 is concentration at initial time and "k" is pseudo first order rate constant. The values of rate constant calculated using pseudo first order equation for the decomposition of both dyes using $BiVO_4$ nanoparticles in visible light radiation were K_{RhB}= 0.006536 min^{-1} and K_{CV}=0.017259 min^{-1} respectively. The results of m-$BiVO_4$ nanoparticles showed admirable photocatalytic activity by maximum adsorption amount. It indicates that catalyst has greater affinity to harvest CV as compared to RhB as shown in Fig. 4.1.6. So, when m-$BiVO_4$ nanoparticles are subjected to visible light irradiation along with organic pollutants (dyes), $BiVO_4$ nanoparticles absorbs radiation, resulting in redox reaction initiation which relate to its optical band gap. As a result, electrons are endorsed from valence band (V_b) to the conduction band (C_b), the electron hole (ehp) pair formed undergo diffusion resulting in redox reaction at the surface of catalyst. The excited Electrons interact with adsorbed O_2 molecules to form superoxide anion radicals ($O_2^{-•}$); on the other hand hole in valance band oxidize OH^- to form the hydroxyl radical species ($^•OH$). The potential of valance band create hydroxyl radicals ($^•OH$) at the $BiVO_4$ surface and potential of conduction band electron adsorbed molecular oxygen leading to peroxide radicals (Niu et al., 2013) as revealed in equations:

$$BiVO_4 + h\upsilon \rightarrow BiVO_4\,[e^- + h^+] \qquad (4.4)$$

$$BiVO_4\,[e^-] + O_2 \rightarrow BiVO_4 + O_2^- \qquad (4.5)$$

$$BiVO_4\,[h^+] + OH^- \rightarrow BiVO_4 + {^•OH} \qquad (4.6)$$

And the overall reaction is

$$BiVO_4 + OH^- + O_2 + OM\ (organic\ matter) \rightarrow BiVO_4 + H_2O + CO_2 \qquad (4.7)$$

As, hydroxyl radical ($^•OH$), is very robust oxidizing agent which hits the "OM" present at the surface of catalyst and oxidize the dye molecules, de-toxic compounds into harmless species, resulting a pure mineral product and CO_2 is released due to the photo degradation process.

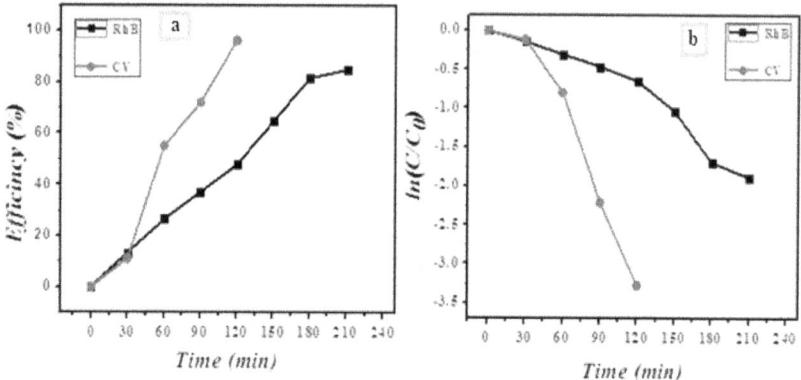

Figure 4.1.6: (a) Degradation efficiency of BiVO$_4$ nanoparticles and **(b)** Photocatalytic degradation analysis by using Pseudo first order equation.

4.1.7 Photoluminescence (PL) analysis

Photoluminescence (PL) spectroscopy is a versatile and widely used to survey the separation efficiency of the charge-carrier, oxygen vacancy, and surface defects in semiconductors. The PL emission intensities of BiVO$_4$ nanoparticles are from the recombination of photo-excited charge-carriers. The room temperature PL emission spectra of pure m-BiVO$_4$ nanoparticles are shown in Fig. 4.1.7. It can be seen that PL spectrum of BiVO$_4$ nanoparticles shows strong emission peaks at 510 and 542nm in the green region, respectively which is in consistent in literature (Ma et al., 2012; Sivakumar et al., 2015). It is perceived that this originate due to the recombination of hole formed in Bi 6s and O 2p and from the electron intuitive in V 3d band. There is blue shift in the emission bands of BiVO$_4$ with that reported for monoclinic BiVO$_4$ at 550nm, which attributed due to particle size and shape properties of the hydrothermally synthesized BiVO$_4$ sample (Lin et al., 2014). It indicates the potential of the m-BiVO$_4$ nanoparticle for visible light devices.

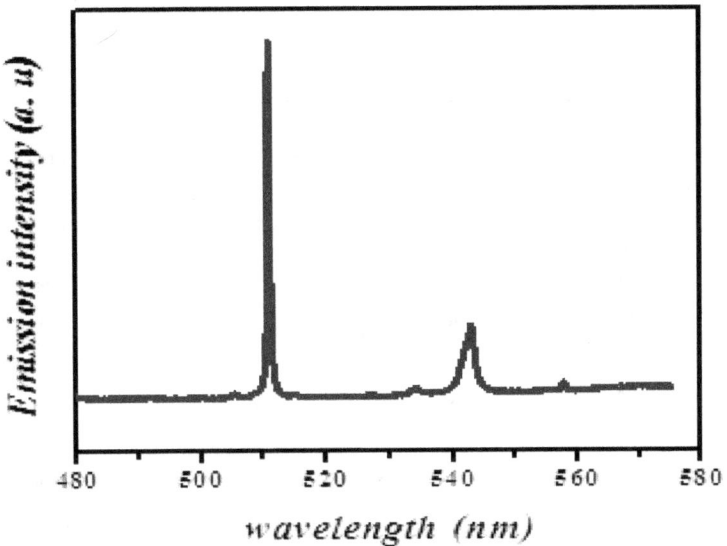

Figure 4.1.7: PL emission spectra of m-BiVO$_4$ at room temperature

Here, Comparison of Photocatalytic activity of some previous reported photocatalysts and present BiVO$_4$ for degradation of Rhodamine-B (RhB) and Crystal violet (CV) are given in table 4.2.

Table 4.2: Comparison of Photocatalytic activity of some previous reported photocatalysts and present BiVO₄ for degradation of Rhodamine-B (RhB) and Crystal violet (CV)

Materials	Dye	Degradation efficiency (%)	Photo-degradation Time	Light source	References
BiVO$_4$ nanoparticles	RhB	82%	180	Visible light	(Moscow et al., 2012)
BiVO$_4$ nanoparticles	RhB	30	5hr	Visible light	(Liu et al., 2011)
BiVO$_4$ nanoparticles	RhB	74	150min	Visible light	(Hofmann et al., 2015)
Ag$_2$Se-G-TiO$_2$	RhB	85.2	180min	Visible light	(Ali et al., 2017)
BWO/1MG	RhB	77.31%	180min	Solar irradiation	(Ming Liu et al., 2017)
BiOI/GR	RhB	80%	240min	Visible light	(Chou, Chung, et al., 2016)
CdS/CdTiO$_3$–TiO$_2$	CV	92.59	180min	Visible light	(Y. Li et al., 2016)
Cd-Al/C	CV	52%	180min	Solar irradiation	(Khan et al., 2016)
Bi$_7$O$_9$I$_3$/GO	CV	96%	1440min	Visible light	(Chou, Chung, et al., 2016)
m-BiVO$_4$ nanoparticles	RhB	84.81%	210 min	Visible light	Present Work
m-BiVO$_4$ nanoparticles	CV	96.23%	120 min	Visible light	Present Work

Section-II

4.2 Enhanced photocatalytic performance of FeVO$_4$ nanoparticles for degradation of Methylene blue dye and industrial waste effluent

4.2.1 Introduction

In this section Ferric vanadate (FeVO$_4$) nanoparticles were synthesized by solution growth single-pot autoclave hydrothermal method with an mean size of 80-90nm. The organized nanoparticles were characterized by X-ray diffraction, FESEM, EDS, UV-visible, FT-IR, BET and photoluminescence (PL) spectroscopy. The photocatalytic activity of the FeVO$_4$ nanoparticles was checked by degradation of Methylene blue (MB) dye and Industrial real waste water under visible light irradiation (400nm < λ < 800nm). FeVO$_4$ nanoparticles showed enhanced photocatalytic performance, can be attributed to novel morphology, BET surface area 89.220 m^{2}g^{-1} verified by applying the Brunauer-Emmett-Teller (BET) technique, narrow band gap 2.73 eV calculated by Tauc's plot from UV-visible spectra and photo-generated electron-hole pair enhanced separation. The photoluminescence spectrum suggests potentials of these nanoparticles in the green visible region of light. Various influence factors, different amount of Hydrogen peroxide (H$_2$O$_2$) lodged which used as an initiator, amount of catalyst, dye concentration, recyclability, and stability was discussed during photocatalysis. It is observed that photo induced degradation activity greatly enhanced for low initiator concentrations than the higher concentration of initiator. This work is helpful for the preparation of FeVO$_4$ and the photocatalytic degradation of the organic pollutants for future applications in water pollution and control.

4.2.2 Scanning Electron Microscopic (SEM) analysis

Figure 4.2.1 depicts the scanning electron micrographs at different magnifications of the as-prepared FeVO$_4$ nanoparticles. Micrographs of FeVO$_4$, captured by SEM showed high surface activity much helpful for photocatalytic degradation of Methylene blue dye. SEM micrograph captured at low magnification endorses the growth of mixed (homogenous and inhomogeneous) shaped and dense nanoparticles, whereas few aggregations and colonies of nanoparticles are noticed at high resolutions. These aggregations may be formed due to inter-particle contacts produced during heat treatment (hydrothermal process). The aggregate size of nanoparticles developed during hydrothermal method is found to be 80-90 nm, which is reported in literature.(Dutta et al., 2017; Hu et al., 2013; Nithya et al., 2011)

Figure 4.2.1: SEM images of the as-synthesized FeVO$_4$ nanoparticles at **(a)** 2μm, 200 KX magnification; **(b)** 200nm, 20000 KX magnification; **(c)** 200nm, 29000 KX magnification and **(d)** 200nm 30000 KX magnification.

4.2.2 Energy Dispersive Spectroscopy (EDX)

Energy dispersive analysis of as-synthesized FeVO$_4$ nanoparticles was employed to estimate the chemical composition of FeVO$_4$. The result of energy dispersive X-ray spectroscopic (EDS) analysis is given in figure 4.2.2. EDS confirm that our as synthesised nanoparticles are consists of only Fe, V and O.

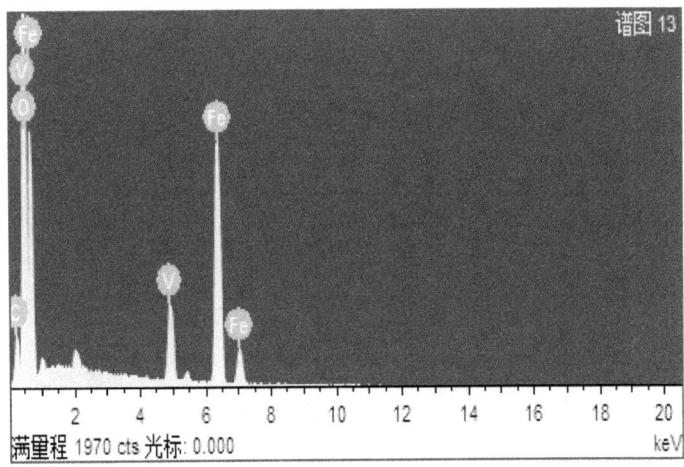

Figure 4.2.2: Energy dispersive analysis of the FeVO$_4$ nanoparticles.

4.2.3 X-Rays Diffraction (XRD)

Figure 4.2.3 shows X-ray diffraction (XRD) spectrum of FeVO$_4$ nanoparticles prepared by hydrothermal method at 180°C for 24 h. All diffraction peaks exhibited in the spectrum of pure FeVO$_4$ Anorthic phase and cell consists of lattice parameters a= 6.7190Å, b=8.0600Å and c= 9.2540Å which are in good agreement with JCPDS (card No. 71-1592). No extra phase is observed in the product.

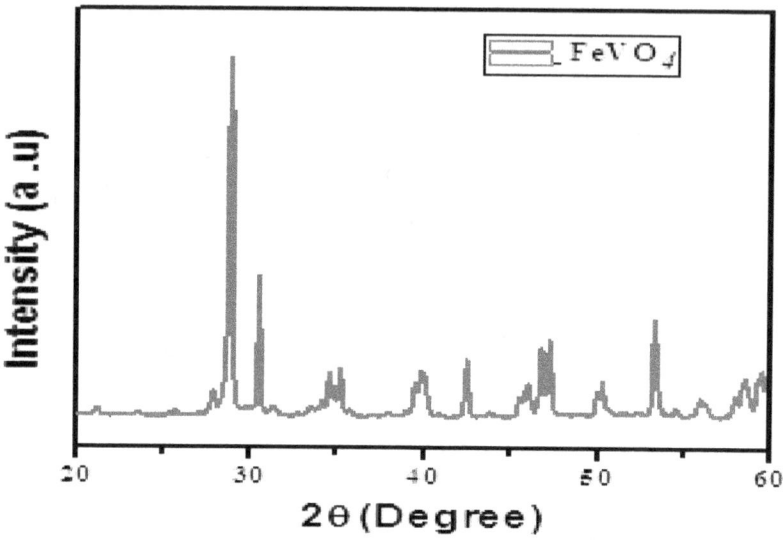

Figure 4.2.3: XRD pattern of the FeVO$_4$ obtained at 180°C for 24 h with the pH ~8.

4.2.4 Fourier Infrared Spectroscopy (FTIR)

FTIR spectrum of FeVO$_4$ nanoparticles is indicated in Figure 4.2.4. Terminal V-O stretching appeared 1054 and 925 cm^{-1}, while the broad peaks at 657 is due to V-O-Fe stretching and V-O-V deformations and Fe-O stretching at 538 and 462 cm^{-1}. characteristic absorption bands due to the V-O terminal, The absorption around 1650 cm^{-1} is due to the bending vibration of water molecules (Vuk et al., 2001) In addition to that, there is a presence of bands at 2966, 2981 and 3463 cm^{-1} that corresponds to CH$_2$ stretching vibrations.(Alagiri et al., 2012)

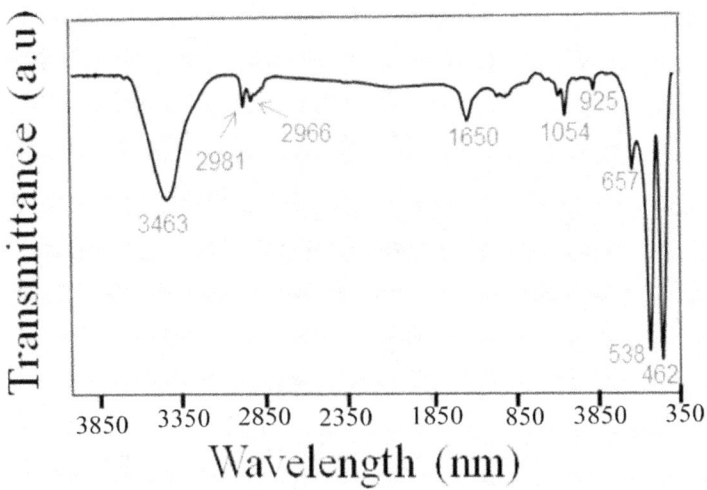

Figure 4.2.4: FTIR spectrum of FeVO$_4$ nanoparticles synthesis at 180°C for 24 hr and pH ~8.

4.2.5 Photocatalytic activity

The photocatalytic responce of the as-grown nanoparticles is studied by the decomposition of methylene blue (MB) in visible light (400 ≤ λ≤ 800nm) illumination. Methylene blue (MB) has wide biological, medical and industrial applications. The chemical structure of methylene blue (MB) used as model dye is given in figure 4.2.5. Hydrogen peroxide (H$_2$O$_2$) with different concentrations is used as reaction initiator in the photocatalytic experiment.

Figure 4.2.5: Structure of Methylene blue (MB) used as sample dye.

The photocatalytic degradation of dye and industrial effluents in the visible light captured with camera indicates the fading of dye color in aqueous media gradually with the passage of time, as shown in Fig. 4.2.6. On the other hand, photocatalytic degradation of MB is not initiated or took too much time to completely degrade the dye solution. It is observed that amount of initiator concentration has a noticeable effect on the photocatalytic degradation activity of nanomaterials. Hydrogen peroxide acts as an electron capture, produces hydroxyl radicals ($^{\bullet}OH$) when exposed to light. The generated $^{\bullet}OH$ radicals being highly oxidant starts the degradation reaction under light irradiation, however, at higher reaction initiator concentrations recombination is dominant. In aqueous medium, hydroxyl radicals are generated by the recombination of hydroxyl groups and holes. The so produced $^{\bullet}OH$ radicals are strong oxidizing agents will oxidize the methylene blue (MB) dye molecules and results in mineralization (H_2O, CO_2) as given in below equation.

$$C_{16}H_{18}ClN_3S + (^{\bullet}OH, \, ^{\bullet}O_2^{-}) \longrightarrow H_2O + CO_2 + NO_2 + SO_2 + C_6H_6$$

The absorption spectra of MB recorded after each 30 min with 0.05 ml of H_2O_2 concentration is shown in Fig. 4.2.6 (a). Decline in the intensity of absorption ranges peaks depicts the decomposition of complex structure of dye by light irradiation.

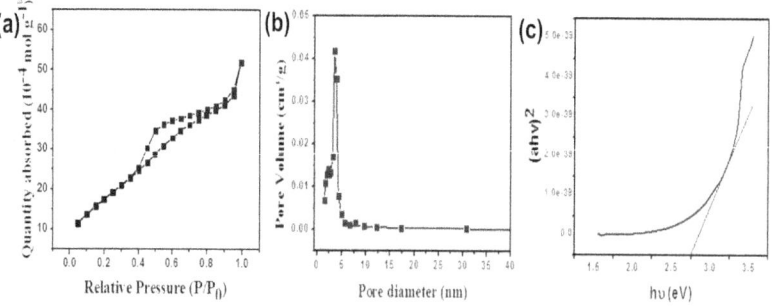

Fig. 4.2.7 (a) shows the BET specific surface area of FeVO$_4$ from nitrogen adsorption-desorption curve (b) differential pore size distribution curve from Barret-Joyner-Halender (BJH) method (c) Band gap calculated by Tauc's plot method

In the present study, we added 0.05 ml, 0.2 ml and 0.3 ml of initiator concentrations dropwise. It is noticed that 0.05 ml of H$_2$O$_2$ has maximum decolonization efficiency as compared to other concentrations. The photocatalytic degradation experiment in the absence of initiator is also conducted, but no or very less degradation activity is observed. A time-dependent photocatalytic experiment is performed to estimate the performance of ferric vanadate (FeVO$_4$) nano-photocatalyst. The characteristic absorption peaks in the presence of different H$_2$O$_2$ concentration decreased gradually with the irradiation time. The effect of higher H$_2$O$_2$ concentrations (0.2 ml and 0.3 ml) for the photocatalytic degradation of dye solution is illustrated, figure 4.2.8 (a–c) and 4.2.9(a–c).

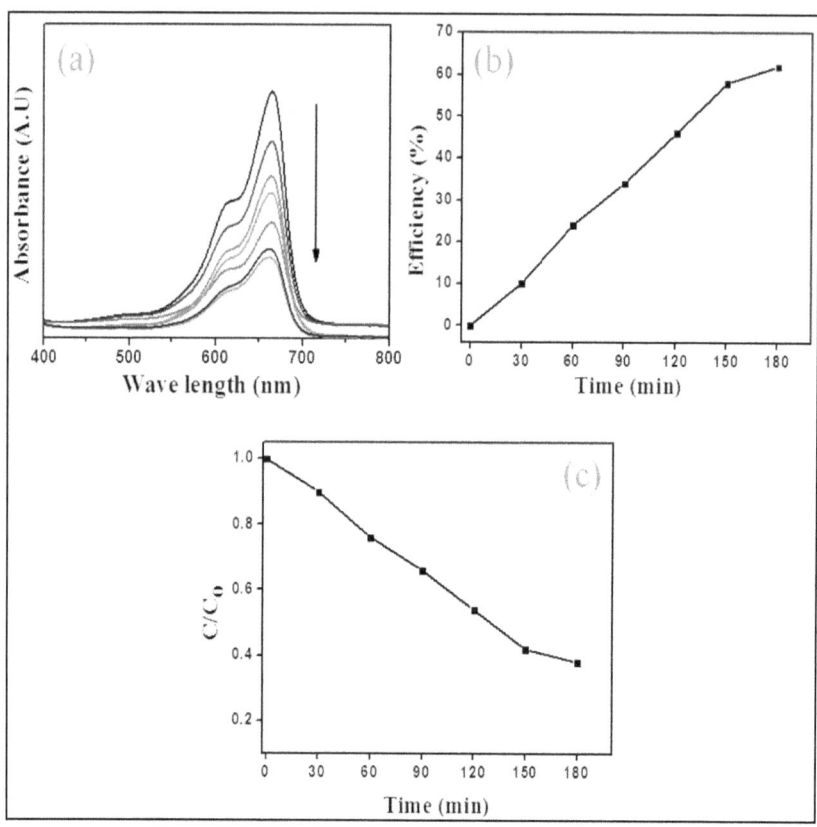

Figure 4.2.8:(a) Photocatalytic degradation of methylene blue (MB) dye when 0.2 ml of reaction initiator (H2O2) is used **(b)** photocatalytic degradation efficiency of NP's **(c)** Degradation analysis.

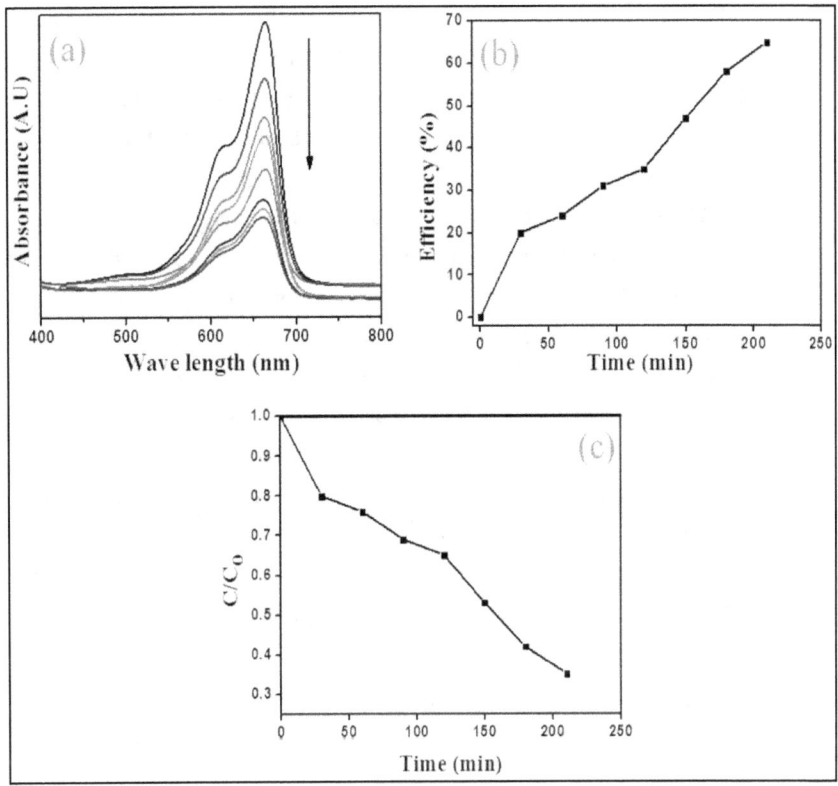

Figure 4.2.9: (a) Photocatalytic degradation of methylene blue (MB) dye when 0.3 ml of reaction initiator (H2O2) is used (b) photocatalytic degradation efficiency of NP's (c) Degradation analysis.

The reaction kinetics is studied using Pseudo first order equation;

$$C/C_o = e^{-kt} \qquad (4.8)$$

Here, C and C_o represents the dye concentration at specific time "t", and at time "t_0", K represents the pseudo first order rate constant. Figure 4.2.9(a-c) represents the reaction kinetics of FeVO$_4$ nanoparticles for the photo-degradation of MB.

Graph between (C/Co) and irradiation time is given in figure 4.2.9c. The value of rate constant calculated by using Pseudo first order equation for 0.05 ml H$_2$O$_2$ is 0.0243 min^{-1}. The rate constant for 0.2 ml & 0.3ml H$_2$O$_2$ is found to be 0.0106 min^{-1} and 0.0082min^{-1}, respectively. It is noticed that solution with lowest initiator concentration has highest degradation efficiency and vice versa. Moreover, very low degradation activity was seen when H_2O_2 was used without $FeVO_4$ nanoparticles, because hydroxyl radicals formed by H_2O_2 hardly continue under visible light.

4.2.6 Brunauer-Emmett-Teller (BET) surface area analysis

The BET measurement is as well implemented to ascertain the surface area of the $FeVO_4$ nanoparticles. The nitrogen adsorption-desorption curve for surface area measurements are depicted in Figure 4.2.10 (a). The particular surface area of $FeVO_4$ is 89.220 m^{2}g^{-1}. The pore size was estimated from desorption isotherms, the Barret-Joyner-Halender (BJH) method (Choi et al., 2015; J.-Q. Li et al., 2014). The estimated pore volume and the average pore diameter are 0.088 cm^{3}g^{-1} and 3.426nm, respectively as shown in Figure 4.2.10(b). Tauc's plot method is used to evaluate the optical band gap as displayed in Figure 4.2.10 (c), the band gap energy as the direct transition is 2.73 eV, which is inconsistent with former reports (Dixit et al., 2011; Mandal et al., 2016; Nong et al., 2015).

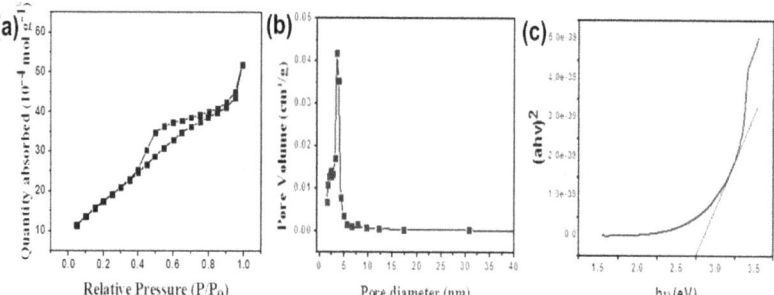

Figure 4.2.10:(a) shows the BET specific surface area of $FeVO_4$ from nitrogen adsorption-desorption curve **(b)** differential pore size distribution curve from Barret-Joyner-Halender (BJH) method **(c)** Band gap calculated by Tauc's plot method.

4.2.7 Photoluminescence (PL)

Photoluminescence (PL) emission spectrum for FeVO4 is shown in Figure 4.2.11; it has well known that photocatalytic efficiency also affected by the photogenerated chargesand their recombination processes. PL emission spectra extensively applied to analyze the recombination rate of free carrier in semiconductor. The PL spectra depict the charge separation and recombination rate within the photocatalysts. The higher the intensity in the PL spectrum, the higher the recombination of electron holes pairs, results in low photocatalytic activity. While the lower PL intensity mean a low recombination rate of electron hole pair which raise efficient separation among photocarriers. Thus, low recombination provides enhance dye degradation efficiency of the photocatalyst. (Fujihara et al., 2000; Hazra et al., 2014; Zhan et al., 2000) FeVO4 show a low emission peak at 624 in red region of visible region of light which corresponds to the transition in Fe–V-oxide. PL study points out the promise of the Ferric vanadate FeVO4 for visible light devices.

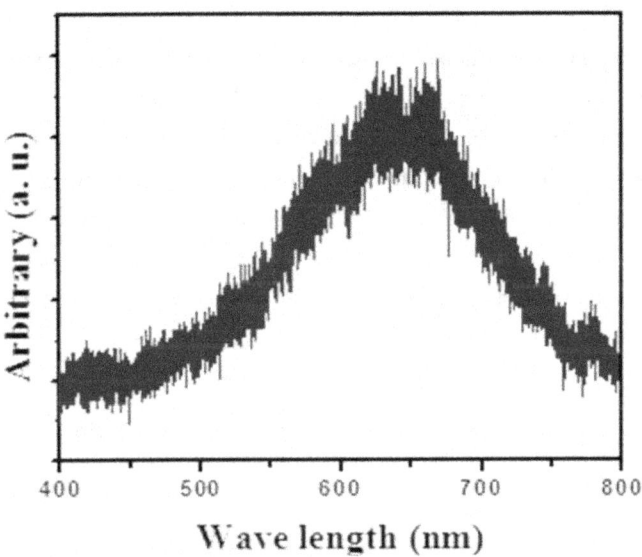

Figure 4.2.11: PL spectrum of $FeVO_4$ nanoparticles at room temperature.

4.2.8 Effect of Dose, stability and recyclability

To evaluate the effect of catalyst amount 0, 5, and 10 mg/10 mL of $FeVO_4$ nanophotocatalyst was dissolved in MB solutions. It was notice that as the concentration was increased the degradation process increases. This implies that the amount of FeVO$_4$ nanophotocatalyst have a significant effect in the photocatalytic reaction for the decomposition of MB. It revealed that at low catalyst dose in the solution, the energy from photo induced electrons could not represent fully utilized, therefore making lower photocatalytic reaction rate. The effect of different dose of FeVO$_4$ nanophotocatalyst for the photocatalytic degradation of dye solution is illustrated, figure 4.2.12. The effect of dye concentration was evaluated by taking different initial concentration of CV dye 10, 20 30 mgL^{-1} and the effect are indicated in figure 4.2.12.

Figure 4.2.12: Effect of the initial dye concentration on photocatalytic degradation of MB.

The degradation efficiency decreases as the amount of dye concentration increase from 10 to 30 mg/L, we consider that when the dye concentration increases it prevents light penetration into the solution and the number of dye molecules increases while the number of ·OH and O radical remain the same under specific conditions on the catalyst surface. Furthermore, the stableness of the FeVO$_4$ nanoparticles photocatalyst was also investigated for 0.05 ml of H$_2$O$_2$ loadage, the photocatalytic degradation process was performed three times and the samples show good stability as shown in figure 4.2.13.

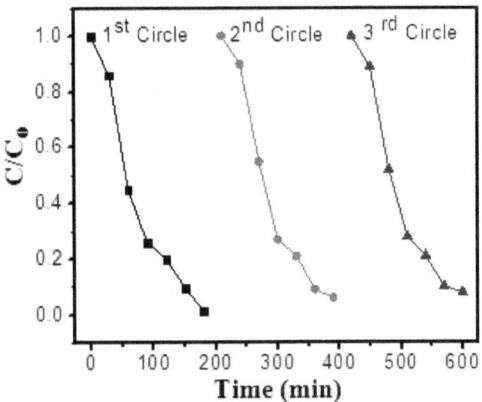

Figure 4.2.13: Stability curves of the photocatalyst FeVO$_4$ for degradation of MB dye

The universality of these nanoparticles was checked for degrading of real coloured wastage water sample. Coloured waste water sample was collected from local textile dyeing industry situated in Beijing region of China. Figure 4.2.14 shows the complete degradation UV-vis spectrum of real waste water sample within 150 min.

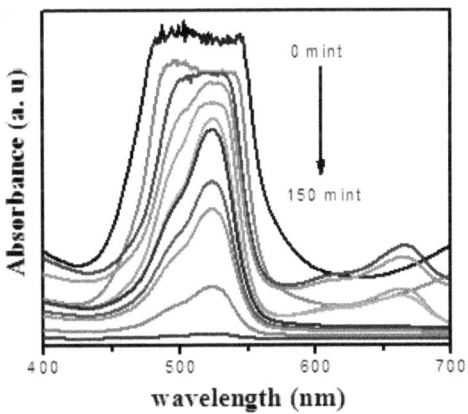

Figure 4.2.14: Uv-visible spectra of real waste water sample.

It was experientially observed FeVO$_4$ with only 0.05 ml of H$_2$O$_2$ exhibited highest photodegradation efficiency as compared to high value of initiator (i.e 0.2

ml and 0.3 ml). This exposes at lowest value of initiator showed the maximum adsorption range and enormous photocatalytic response.

Here, Comparison of Photocatalytic activity of some previous reported photocatalysts and present $FeVO_4$ for degradation of Methylene blue (MB) under visible light irradiation is given in table 4.3.

Table: 4.3 Comparison of Photocatalytic activities of some photocatalysts and Current $FeVO_4$ for degradation of Methylene blue (MB) under visible light irradiation.

Materials	Degradation efficiency (%)	Time	References
$V_2O_3/CNT/TiO_2$	70	2 hr	47
$CuO-BiVO_4$	92	5 hr	48
ZnS/CdS	73	6 hr	49
$ZnFe_2O_4$	95	3 hr	50
ZnS	88	90 min	51
$BiVO_4/TiO_2$	86	2 hr	52
$BiVO_4$	67.21	4 hr	53
$BiVO_4$ wrapped in Graphene	95	210 min	54
$PoPD/TiO_2$	44.5	3 hr	55
V_2O_5	81	2 hr	56
$FeVO_4$	98.74	180 min	Present Work

Section-III

4.3 Facile Synthesis of Zinc Vanadate $Zn_3(VO_4)_2$ for highly efficient visible light assisted Photocatalytic activity

4.3.1 Introduction

In the preceding section Zinc Vanadate $Zn_3(VO_4)_2$ nanoplates with width and thickness 300 ~ 500 nm and 50 ~ 7 nm diameter were synthesized by the facile modified hydrothermal method. Which containing mixing of Ammonia metavanadate (NH_4VO_3) powder with zinc acetate [$Zn(CH_3COO)_2.2H_2O$], in the presence of CTAB and N, N-dimethyl formamide (DMF), the pH was adjusted around 5 and white precipitates were obtained. The potential of $Zn_3(VO_4)_2$ photocatalyst was investigated by degrading Congo Red (CR) and Crystal Violet (CV) dyes using a UV-visible spectrophotometer. These Zinc vanadate nanoplates (ZnVO-Nps) showed enhanced dye removal (100%) due to reduced band gap 2.68eV and high surface area (84m²/g). The Photoluminescence measurement showed the ZnVO-Nps potential for blue/green visible optical devices. These result showed that ZnVO-Nps have higher photocatalytic degradation owing to the high level surface area and absorbency; it is proposed that the ZnVO-Nps demonstrated the high-level application for the deprivation of organic contaminants in visible light illuminations.

4.3.2 Scanning Electron Microscopy (SEM)

SEM micrographs of as-prepared $Zn_3(VO_4)_2$ nanoplates are displayed in Figure 4.3.1 shows cross-sectional and top sight SEM images taken at low magnification while images (inset) taken at high magnification, display nanoplates with width and thickness 300 ~ 500nm and 50 ~ 75nm. Our results resemble in literature with yaungyu et al., who synthesized pyrovanadate nanosheets by hydrothermal method at 200°C with width 400–500nm and its thickness is nearly about 100nm (Yu et al., 2016). It is perceived that this formation of nanoplates is because of chelation of metal cations in the solution.

Figure 4.3.1: SEM image at low magnification, and high magnification of $Zn_3(VO_4)_2$ nanoplates hydrothermally synthesized at 180°C.

4.3.3 Energy Dispersive Spectroscopy (EDX)

Energy dispersive X-ray spectroscopic (EDX) technique was exercised to evaluate the chemical composition of $Zn_3(VO_4)_2$ nanoplates. The result of EDX investigation is displayed in Figure 4.3.2. It confirms that $Zn_3(VO_4)_2$ consists of only Zn, O, and V. No other impurity is detected in the obtained product within the detection limit. The atomic ratio was found to be 14.12:28.61:57.27, which closed to the stoichiometric ratio of $Zn_3(VO_4)_2$.

Figure 4.3.2: EDX analysis of $Zn_3(VO_4)_2$ nanoplates synthesis at 180°C.

4.3.4 X-Rays Diffraction (XRD)

The synthesized ZnVO-Nps were further characterized using X-ray powder diffraction method for phase purity as shown in Figure 4.3.3. The intense peaks reflect strong crystal quality of $Zn_3(VO_4)_2$, the strongest peak at position 34.33 All the peaks matched well with listed together with JCPDS No. 11-0288 and no secondary phase or impurity peaks were observed indicating the phase purity of the obtained product, which is consistent with previously reported results in the literature.

Figure 4.3.3: The XRD pattern for the as-synthesized $Zn_3(VO_4)_2$ nanoplates at 180°C.

4.3.5 X-ray photoelectron spectroscopy (XPS)

XPS is a versatile tool for the evaluation of chemical composition and purity of the product so for further superficial chemical analysis of the $Zn_3(VO_4)_2$ nanoplates was examined by XPS, Figure 4.3.4 (a) Indicating the obtained results as it can be seen from the XPS spectrum that our sample is composed of Zn, V, and O elements. The binding energies of Zn 2p core levels from resolution XPS spectra revealed at 1021.4 and 1044.60 eV for Zn $2p_{3/2}$ and Zn $2p_{1/2}$ of this sample as indicated in Figure. 4.3.4 (b), 517.13 and 524.64 eV for V $2p_{3/2}$ and V$2p_{1/2}$ as shown in Figure 4.3.4 (c), and for O 2s the typical 530.4 eV was observed as represented in Figure 4.3.4(d), respectively. These results are in good consistent with those reported.(Guo et al., 2014; Ni et al., 2010; Pitale et al., 2012)From the above detailed XPS spectra peaks, the outputs from XRD, EDX confirming the products are pure $Zn_3(VO_4)_2$.

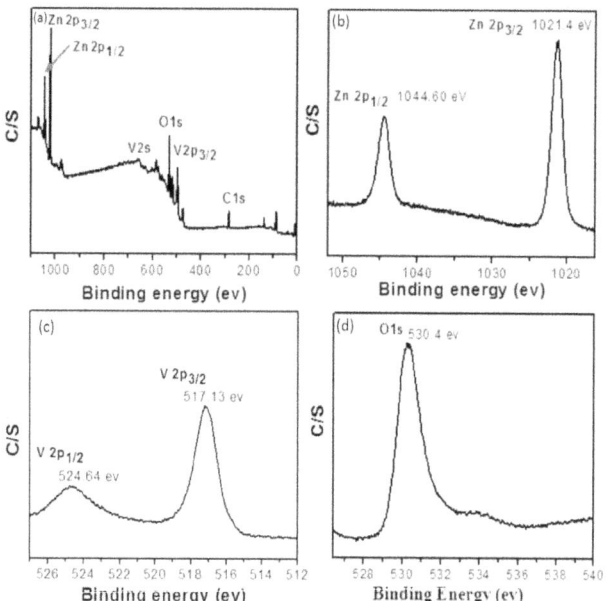

Figure 4.3.4:(a) wide scan total XPS spectrum of the $Zn_3(VO_4)_2$ nanoplates sample, **(b)** ForZn 2p; **(c)** For V 2p and **(d)** For O 1s.

4.3.6 Fourier Infrared spectroscopy (FTIR)

FTIR spectrum of $Zn_3(VO_4)_2$ nanoplates is shown in Figure 4.3.5. The peaks at 455 cm^{-1} and 996 cm^{-1}, are allotted to symmetric (V–O–Zn) and (V–O–V) while peaks at 774 cm^{-1} are attributing to asymmetric (V–O–Zn) and (V–O–V). The peaks at 1625 cm−1, 3481 cm^{-1} is indorsed due to the stretching and bending vibration of H–O–H from H_2O molecule absorbed by the surface of the $Zn_3(VO_4)_2$ plates. These peaks are consistent with the previously reported values.

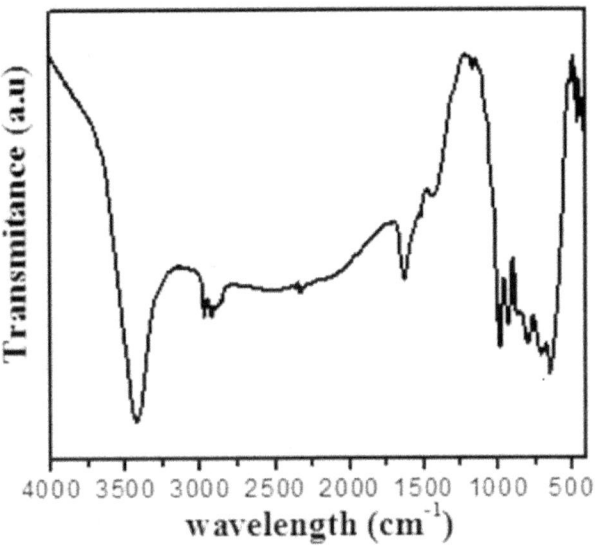

Figure 4.3.5: FTIR spectrum of the as-prepared $Zn_3(VO_4)_2$ nanoplates.

4.3.7 Photocatalytic activity

The photocatalytic mechanism typically contains three steps: absorption of a photon having energy equal or greater than photocatalyst band gap energy, second generation and recombination of electron-hole pairs, number three and finally Oxidation and reduction occurrences at photocatalyst surface. Schematic representation for the creation of holes and electrons in the $Zn_3(VO_4)_2$ nanomaterial upon imposing visible light for successive mineralization of CR and CV dyes is shown in Figure 4.3.6. When photons of energy equable/higher than its band-gap energy of photocatalyst, it interacts with photocatalyst and electron-hole (ehp) pairs are generated and separated. The excited electron reacts with adsorbate oxygen specks O_2 to make electronically involved superoxide anion radicals ($O_2^{\cdot -}$). Although the stimulated holes in the valance band oxidize $^-$OH preceding to the generation of hydroxyl radical species ($^{\cdot}$OH), (Zhang et al., 2018) this hydroxyl $^{\cdot}$OH radical being a very robust oxidizing agent would oxidize the dye molecules to the mineral remaining products, i.e. CO_2, H_2O.(Sajid et al., 2018)

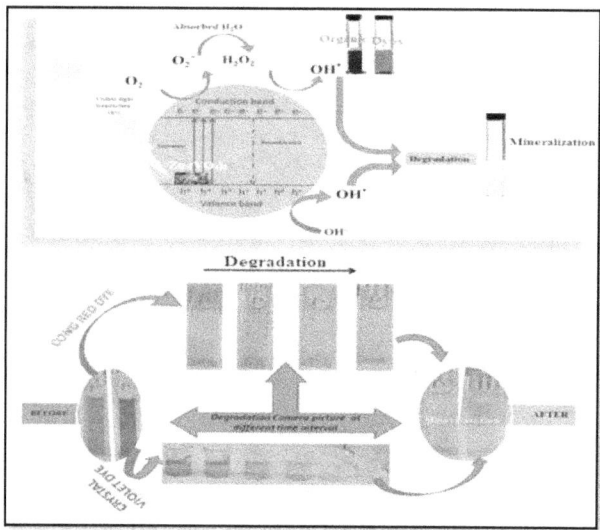

Figure 4.3.6: Photocatalysis mechanism for the degradation of dyes.

The BET surface area was evaluated by Brunauer-Emmett-Teller (BET, ASAP-2020) using adsorption isotherms in relative pressure at (P/P$_o$) ranges from 0.05 to 0.25, the BET surface area of ZnVO-Nps is 84 m^2/g, which is obviously high, owing to regular orientation of pores in the structure and showing highly crystalline nature of nanoplates.(G. Yang et al., 2016) $Zn_3(VO_4)_2$ nanoplates possessing large surface area represents a higher tendency to adsorb dyes which improve the response of photocatalytic degradation for the dyes. The pore size was calculated by desorption isotherms, the Barret-Joyner-Halender (BJH) method, (Fatima et al., 2017; Irfan, Li, et al., 2017; Irfan,

Shen, et al., 2017) an average pore size of 9nm can be seen from the differential pore size distribution curve in inset of Figure 4.3.7(a), The pore size dispersion of powder displays intense peak about 4nm to 6nm, due to antiparticle gaps, and nonporous in the fabrications of $Zn_3(VO_4)_2$ nanoplates. This type of uniformly homogenous well defined nonporous structure is suitable for photocatalysis as it offers effective pathways to reactant molecules and byproducts. BET results prove that the hysteresis is the H_3 type which associates with slit shape capillaries having wide frames and reduced stems of plate-like group atoms. The lamellar pore slit shape pores construction clearly indicates the presence of mesopores within the structure. Thus, the $Zn_3(VO_4)_2$ oxide is an extremely highly crystalline mesopores material. Tauc's plot method used to calculate ZnVO-Np optical band gap of 2.68 eV as shown in Figure 4.3.7(b), which is quite similar to the previouslyreported.(LZ Pei et al., 2015)

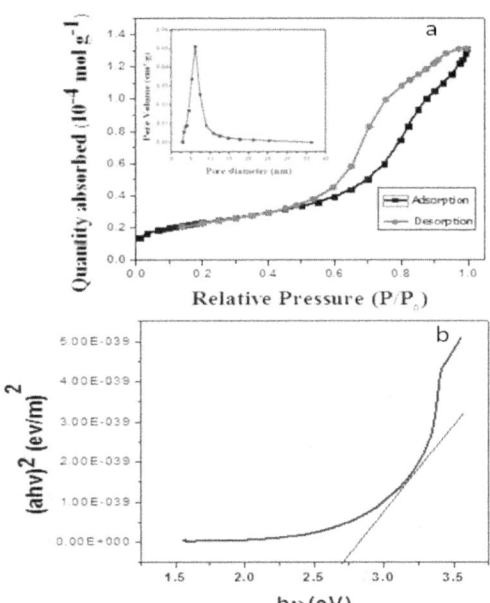

Figure 4.3.7:(a) Nitrogen adsorption-desorption curve for surface area measurement of $Zn_3(VO_4)_2$ nanoplates **(b)** Tauc plot for $Zn_3(VO_4)_2$ composite

Congo red ($C_{32}H_{22}N_6Na_2O_6S_2$) is a benzene derivative dye known carcinogenic compound and extensively used to treat leather articles, textiles and some foods. It has a harmful effect on human, aquatic life as well as on land. Crystal violet ($C_{25}H_{30}ClN_3$) is the mixture of tetramethyl, pentamethyl, hexamethyl and pararosanilines, commonly used in textile industries for colour purposes. It is poisonous in nature because it yields toxic output as carbon monoxide, carbon dioxide, nitrogen oxides and hydrogen chlorides and has harmful effects on human, agricultural and on aquatic life. (Chen et al., 2018; Lee et al., 2019) The photocatalytic reaction of as-synthesized ZnVO-Nps was evaluated by photocatalytic degradation of CR and CV dyes under visible light irradiation. The chemical structure of Congo red and crystal violet is shown in Figure 4.3.8.

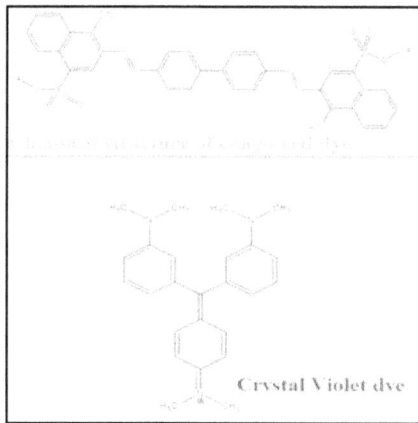

Figure 4.3.8: Chemical Structure of Congo red (CR) and Crystal Violet (CV) dyes.

For a photocatalytic response, the ZnVO-Nps have been used to the degradation of CR and CV organic dyes under Visible radiation; for comparison, the photocatalytic response of CR and CV was also investigated by the usage of ZnVO-Nps without visible light and visible light without ZnVO-Nps catalyst, individually. The initial Congo red, Crystal violet and ZnVO-Nps concentration are 10 mg/L CR, 10 mg/L CV and 10 mg/10 mL solution, separately.

The typical absorption peak from Congo Red (CR) is turned up at 496nm, Similarly, the peculiar absorption peak of CV is situated at 582nm. The intensity level of the peak decreased evidently on the increase in time of the visible light illumination. Congo red dye concentration step-downs to 0 mg/L after visible light irradiating for 2.5h. The colour of CR dye solution transfers from bright Red to colourless, we repeated the photocatalytic experiment for three times and the evaluated error bar is inserted in 10(c). Figure 4.3.9(a) indicates the CV absorption ratio subsequently at classified interval conditions. The CV C/Co ratio decreased to zero within 60 mints. The colour of the CV solution alters from deep blue to colourless each time as we repeated the experiment for three times, the error bar graph is illustrated in Figure 4.3.9(c).

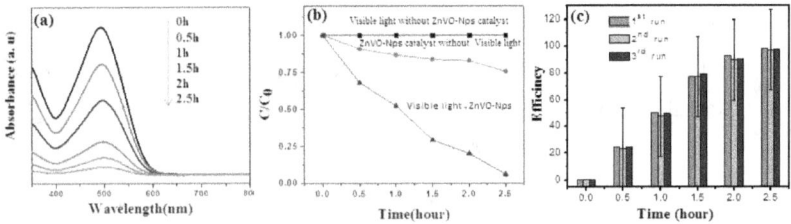

Figure 4.3.9: (a) Absorption bands of CR solution at illuminated times taking 50mL CR solution under visible light, (b) CR concentration ratio treated with ZnVO-Nps solution at different irradiation time, (c) Error bar graph for photocatalytic measurement of CR solution.

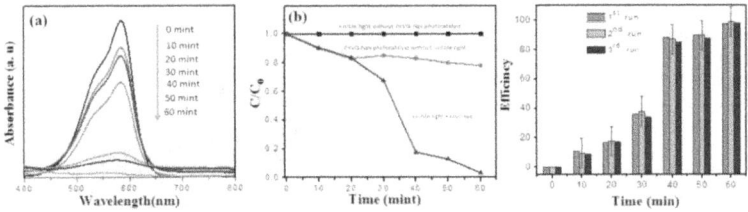

Figure 4.3.10: (a) Absorption spectra of CV solution at different interval carrying 10mL CV solution under visible light, (b) CV concentration ratio treated with ZnVO-Nps solution at different irradiation time, (c) Error bar graph for photocatalytic measurement of CV solution.

To realize the role of the visible light on the photocatalytic reaction for Congo red and crystal violet dye, the degradation percentage was also evaluated under visible light without any photocatalyst. From the Figure (4.3.9b, 4.3.10b) it can be seen that there is no photocatalytic activity for both dyes solution with visible light without ZnVO-Nps. On the other hand, the ZnVO-Nps bear very little photocatalytic response for dyes without visible light irradiation. The graphical record between C/Co ratio and radiation time as Figure 4.3.9(b) and 4.3.10(b) shows the CR photodegradation is about 25.31 in 2.5 h and CV photodecompose ratio represents nearly 22.06% in 60 mints respectively. Thus, it's evident that the photocatalytic activities for CR and CV degradation are specific by visible light radiation assisted.(Irfan, Shen, et al., 2017; LZ Pei et al., 2015) The photocatalytic reaction considered to be related particularly activated kind of peroxide (O_2^-) then hydroxyl ($^\cdot OH$) created from electrons and holes coming to the surface of the water.(Mao et al., 2008) When the ZnVO-Nps oxidize the water due to low band gap the activation energy instantly overcome the band hole using ZnVO-Nps and give superior photocatalytic efficiency under visible radiation.

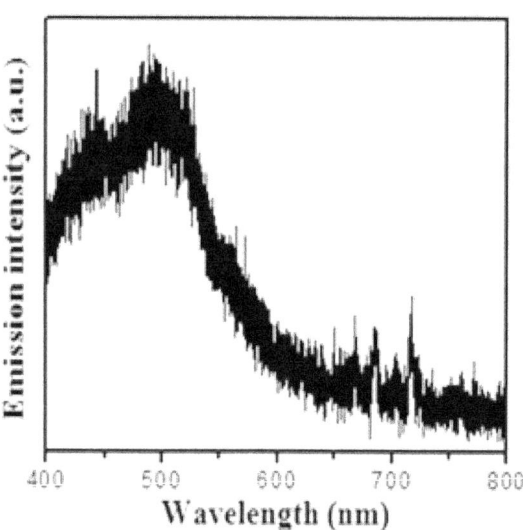

Figure 4.3.11: Photoluminescence (PL) spectrum of ZnVO-Nps at room temperature.

4.3.8 Photoluminescence (PL)

Figure 4.3.11 shows the PL spectra of $Zn_3(VO_4)_2$ nanoplates evaluated at room temperature applying the excitation wavelength of 325nm. Strong emission spectra from 480 to 550nm are obtained in the PL spectrum. The blue emission centre placed at 492 (2.52 eV). It is found from the previous PL literature survey that Zinc vanadate show new energy levels inside the band gap of nanostructures that can be stimulated by Zn-vacancy, O-vacancy, zinc interstitial and O⁻ interstitial. This type of Vacancies produce newly energy levels in the bandgap of nanomaterials; these new energy levels are called deep energy levels (DEL). (M. Wang et al., 2012; L.-L. Yang et al., 2009) The sharp and strong peak might be due to these new vacancies or defects which are attributed due to the charge transition in the VO_4 tetrahedra due to defects/vacancies. (Ahmad et al., 2010; Liu et al., 2013) This PL study endows the promise of $Zn_3(VO_4)_2$ with nanoplates morphology could be an excellent candidate for blue/green visible light emitting devices, in the optical and another field. Diffusion of the ehp charge carry on at the surface of the ZnVO-Nps and the photocatalytic reactions may be described as in following equations.(Pei et al., 2013)

$$ZnVO\text{-}Nps + h\nu \qquad ZnVO\text{-}Nps\ (e^- + h^+) \qquad (4.9)$$
$$H_2O + h^+ \qquad OH^- + H^+ \qquad (4.10)$$
$$O_2 + e^- \qquad O^{-2} \qquad (4.11)$$

The photocatalytic degradation method of the ZnVO-Nps is the direct absorption procedure of a photon with the aid of the energy band gap. It is well-known that photocatalytic response may be additionally affected by the competition between recombination and the charge separation approaches and photoluminescence emission spectra had been extensively used to observe the rate of charge recombination. (F.-Y. Liu, Y.-R. Jiang, et al., 2018; F.-Y. Liu, J.-H. Lin, et al., 2018b)

Here, Comparison of Photocatalytic activity of some previous reported photocatalysts and present $Zn_3(VO_4)_2$ for degradation of CR and CV dye under visible light irradiation is given in table 4.4.

Table: 4.4: Comparison of Photocatalytic activity of some photocatalysts and Current $Zn_3(VO_4)_2$ for degradation of CR and CV dye under visible light irradiation.

Powder	Dye	Efficiency	Time	Reference
P-25, Degussa	CR	85%	240 mint	(de Souza et al., 2014)
P-25, Degussa	CR	87.9%	180 mint	(Anku et al., 2016)
P-25, Degussa	CR	67%	120 mint	(Narayan et al., 2011)
P-25, Degussa	CR	88 %	165 mint	(Kar et al., 2015)
Fe_3O_4/CuO	CR	99%	300 mint	(Malwal et al., 2016)
SnO_2/CdS	CR	97%	240 mint	(Kar et al., 2012)
$Zn_3(VO_4)_2$ nanoplates	CR	100%	150 mint	Present Work
P-25, Degussa	CV	49%	60 mint	(Adhikari et al., 2016)
ZnO	CV	95%	300 mint	(Shinde et al., 2017)
$CdS/CdTiO_3$–TiO_2	CV	61%	180 mint	(Y. Li et al., 2016)
Ag_3VO_4/g-C3N4	CV	34%	150 mint	(Lam et al., 2016)
Cd-Al/C	CV	52%	180mint	(Khan et al., 2016)
$Bi_7O_9I_3$/GO	CV	96%	1440 mint	(Chou, Chung, et al., 2016)
$Zn_3(VO_4)_2$ Nanoplates	CV	100%	60 mint	Present Work

Section-IV

4.4 Synthesis of BiVO$_4$/FeVO$_4$ nanocomposite for enhanced photocatalytic degradation of CV dye and electrochemical detection of Ascorbic acid

4.4.1 Introduction

In this section, BiVO$_4$/FeVO$_4$ nanocomposite photocatalyst were well produced by hydrothermal system. The synthesised heterojunction photocatalyst were characterized physically and chemically via XRD, SEM, EDX, XPS, BET, FT-IR, Raman, UV-vis DRS, EPR and Photoluminescence technique. BiVO$_4$/FeVO$_4$ was explored for their photocatalytic activity measurement by decomposition of crystal violet (CV) organic dye under visible radiation. It indicated that BiVO$_4$/FeVO$_4$ completely degrades CV within 60 min at ratio 2:1. In addition, BiVO$_4$/FeVO$_4$ was as well investigated for electrochemical detection of useful analyte ascorbic acid using electrochemical impedance spectroscopy (EIS) and cyclic voltammetry techniques. This work displays the potential of BiVO$_4$/FeVO$_4$ nanocomposite for applications in environmental discipline as well as in biosensor sciences.

4.4.2 X-Rays Diffraction (XRD) and Energy Dispersive Spectroscopy (EDX)

Figure 4.4.1(a); shows the XRD diffraction pattern of as-prepared BiVO$_4$/FeVO$_4$nanophotocatalyst at different concentration ratios for phase structures. The XRD diffraction peaks of BiVO$_4$/FeVO$_4$ are in agreement to pure BiVO$_4$ (JCPD card 85-1730)(Gao et al., 2017) and to FeVO$_4$ (JCPD card 24-0541) thus, the pattern of BiVO$_4$/FeVO$_4$ hetero-junction photocatalyst compound displayed typical diffraction peaks from both BiVO$_4$ and FeVO$_4$ distinct phases, verified that BiVO$_4$/FeVO$_4$ nanocomposite prepared successfully by autoclave hydrothermal process at different mole ratio as shown from figure 4.4.1(a). The intense and edged peaks of BiVO$_4$ suggest the bigger crystallite size, as, the small peaks of ferric vanadate indicating small-scale particle size. There is a shift in peaks (Fig. 4.4.1b) first towards left when concentration is 2:1 and peaks shifts towards right as concentration increases 5:1 to 10:1, colour is found. The colour also changes gradually into yellowish as BiVO$_4$concentration is increased. It can be clearly observed that the broadening of BiVO$_4$ peaks takes places and the intensity of FeVO$_4$ peaks declines. Here it is observed that optimum conditions for making BiVO$_4$/FeVO$_4$ (2:1) at which high intensity and intense peaks are found as it is indicated in figure 4.38a. For chemical analysis the EDS analysis is shown in figure 4.4.1c, it's observed that the elements, Vanadium, Iron, Bismuth, and Oxygen are homogeneously spread in composite, the presence of carbon and platinum peaks are due to carbon tape and Pt. coating. Beside this, no impurities have been detected within detection limit.

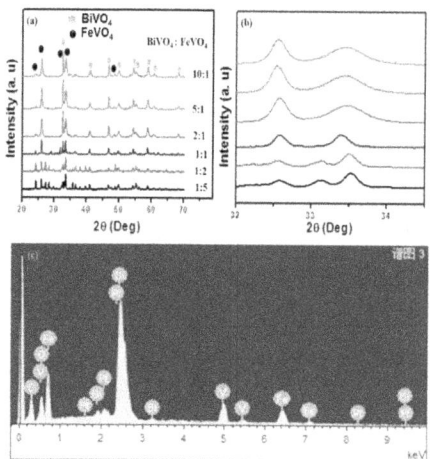

Figure 4.4.1: **(a)** XRD spectrum of BiVO$_4$/FeVO$_4$ composite heterojunction photocatalyst at different mole ratio 1:5, 1:2, 1:1, 2:1, 5:1 and 10:1; **(b)** Peaks shifts in the XRD spectrum of BiVO$_4$/FeVO$_4$ by increasing concentration of BiVO$_4$**(c)** EDS analysis of BiVO$_4$/FeVO$_4$ composite at mole ratio 2:1

4.3.5 Scanning Electron Microscopy (SEM)

The surface topography and morphological analysis of BiVO$_4$/FeVO$_4$ nanocomposite were characterized by field emission scanning electron microscopy, JEOL-7001F. SEM images at different concretion (1:5, 1:2, 1:1, 2:1, 5:1 and 10:1) are illustrated in figure 4.4.2(a-f). It was noticed that at higher concentration of FeVO$_4$ the small size nanocomposite are developed as shown in figure 4.4.2a and 4.4.2b when the concentration of BiVO$_4$/FeVO$_4$ was 1:5, the rod and particle shaped nanostructures were formed,. While at concentration 1:2 the polyhedrons and particles shaped nanostructure formation occurred. In the opposite case as we increase the mole ratio of BiVO$_4$ in the BiVO$_4$/FeVO$_4$ nanocomposite the large crystallite size were found as shown in figure 4.4.2(d-f). In figure 4.4.2(d) the BiVO$_4$/FeVO$_4$ nanocomposite at mole ratio 2:1 comprises road, plate, and some plate are linked with each other to form ply chain and looked like flower type structure. At mole ratio 5:1 the SEM image captured showed the rod and plate-like structures in which the agglomerations of plates are more than the previous concentration ratio. The SEM image in fig 4.4.2(f) of the BiVO$_4$/FeVO$_4$ nanocomposite at mole ratio 10:1 showed flowers and just a few plates structures are found respectively.

Figure 4.4.2: SEM images of BiVO$_4$/FeVO$_4$ composite heterojunction photocatalyst at different mole ratio **(a)** 1:5, **(b)** 1:2, **(c)** 1:1, **(d)** 2:1, **(e)** 5:1 and **(f)** 10:1.

4.4.3 X-ray photoelectron spectroscopy (XPS)

XPS is a practiced surface analysis method for investigating the composition and chemical states of constituents. in order to validate further the elemental analysis is carried out by performing XPS characterization Figure 4.4.3(a) shows the typical X-ray photoelectron spectrum of the $BiVO_4/FeVO_4$ nanocomposite is composed of O, Bi, V, and Fe. The XPS analysis of $BiVO_4/FeVO_4$ nanocomposite (2:1) is showed (Fig.4.4.3), two peaks of Oxygen at 1s are located at 530.6 and 531.8 eV (Wang et al., 2015; Wang et al., 2014) in Fig. 4.4.3(b) showing the two different peaks of O in the experiment. Two peaks of V $2p_{3/2}$ at 517.41 eV and V $2p_{1/2}$ at 524.12 eV were noticed, respectively as in Fig. 4.4.3(c). Fig. 4.4.3(d) indicates the XPS peaks of Bi $4f_{7/2}$ and Bi $4f_{5/2}$, found at 159.44 eV and 164.68 eV(Gu et al., 2015). Fig. 4.4.3(e), the Fe 2p spectra were compiled of two leading peaks ($2p_{1/2}$ and $2p_{3/2}$) with many sub-peaks, the main peaks positioned at 711.27 and 725.19 eV (Yang et al., 2015), respectively. The peaks shift was found as same in XRD analysis may be attributed due to morphology effect or increasing concentration of $BiVO_4$. From above XRD and XPS detailed spectra showing the confirm formation of $BiVO_4/FeVO_4$ heterojunction photocatalyst.

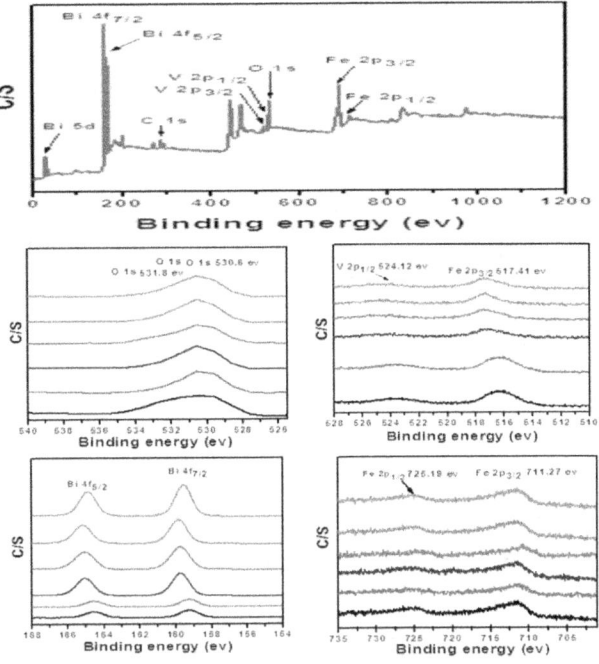

Figure 4.4.3: XPS of BiVO$_4$/FeVO$_4$ nanocomposite at different mole ratios of BiVO$_4$ and FeVO$_4$.

4.4.4 Brunauer–Emmett–Teller (BET) Surface area

The N$_2$ sorption isotherms of nanocomposite photocatalyst BiVO$_4$/FeVO$_4$ (2:1) was produced and examined. The Brunauer–Emmett–Teller surface area was to be 70.147 cm^{2}g^{-1}. The pore size was estimated from desorption isotherms, the Barret-Joyner-Halender (BJH) method (Chung et al., 2017; Imam et al., 2018). The evaluated pore volume and the average pore diameter are 0.124 cm^{3}g^{-1} and 3.798nm, respectively as shown in figure 4.4.4. The adsorption curve is a type III curve presenting the hysteresis of H$_2$ and H$_3$ types, which associates slit shape capillaries with large and narrow short plate-like aggregates of particles resulting in lamellar pore structure and slit Shape pores (Khan et al., 2017). The lamellar pore wedged shape pores construction clearly indicates the presence of mesopores within the structure. The Brunauer–Emmett–Teller surface area of $BiVO_4/FeVO_4$ composite at mole ratio (1:5, 1:2, 1:1, 5:1, 10:1) was 136.188, 6.019, 7.097, 9.325, 14.679 cm2g-1 pore volume 0.213, 0.010, 0.012, 0.013, 0.025 cm^3g^{-1} and pore diameter 1.682, 1.932, 1.682, 1.937 and 2.181nm respectively, as shown in figure 4.4.5.

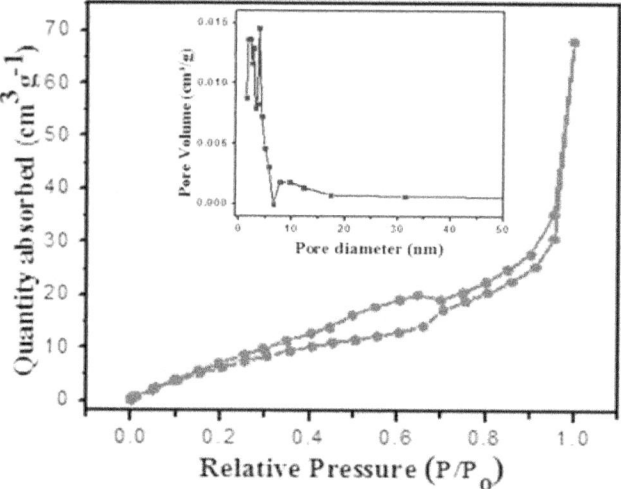

Figure 4.4.4: BET surface area (inset pore diameter) of 2:1 $BiVO_4/FeVO_4$ composite at 77.35 K.

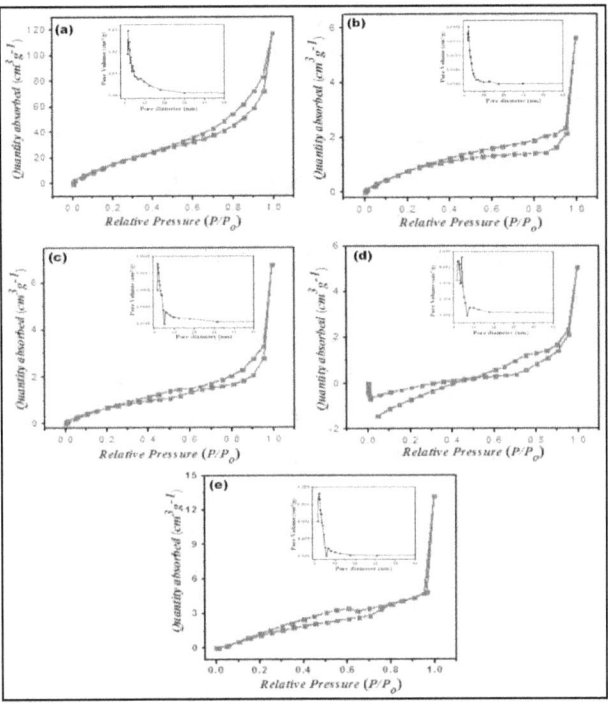

Figure 4.4.5: Show the N_2 gas isotherms at 77.5 K of $BiVO_4/FeVO_4$ nanocomposite at a different mole ratio at **(a)** 1:5 **(b)** 1:2 **(c)** 1:1 **(d)** 5:1 and **(e)** 10:1 the BET surface area and BJH pore size in inset.

4.4.5 Fourier Infrared Spectroscopy (FTIR)

Fig. 4.4.6(a) shows the FT-IR spectra of the $BiVO_4/FeVO_4$ heterogeneous composite prepared under different mole ratio, where the absorption from 3000 to 3600 cm^{-1} due to the stretching vibration of OH bound of absorbed water. The absorption at 1631 unit is due to absorbed water molecule bending vibration. The band at 512 cm^{-1} is of V-O-V deformation causes due to Fe-O stretching mode. The peaks 741, 837, 915 and 1052 cm-1 correspond to V=O and V–O–V joined vibrations and the stretching of short vanadyl bond, While Bi–O bending and asymmetric vibration appeared at 474 cm^{-1}, 1362 cm^{-1}, respectively (Alagiri et al.,

2012; Ghiyasiyan-Arani et al., 2018; Lee et al., 2017; Pookmanee et al., 2014; Vuk et al., 2001).

4.4.6 Raman Analysis

Raman analysis is a useful tool to provide structural information and is also a sensitive method for the investigating of the crystallization, local structure, as well as for electronic dimensions of materials. In figure 4.4.6(b), Raman bands around 198, 333, 367, 640, and 836 cm^{-1} were observed for all samples that correspond to BiVO$_4$ while bands around 139, 300, 354, 655, 962 and 996 cm^{-1} represent FeVO$_4$ in the samples (Lehnen et al., 2014; Merupo et al., 2015; Nikam et al., 2016). The shift in the peaks was observed, as concentration mole ratio changed, at higher concentration of BiVO$_4$ its peaks become broader and cover FeVO$_4$ peaks, as it was observed in XRD and XPS analysis which also confirmed our previous result.

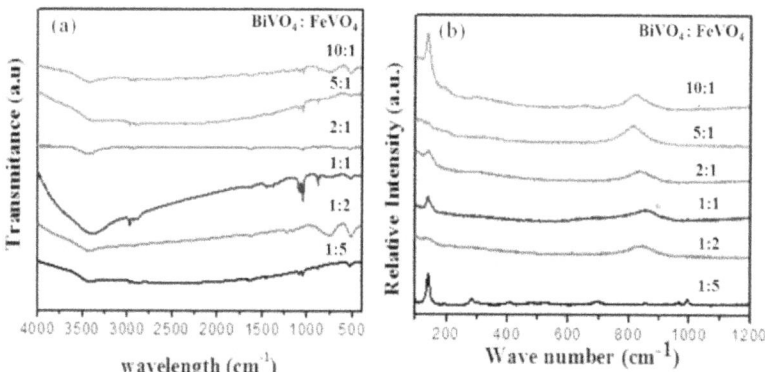

Figure 4.4.6: (a) FTIR spectra and (b) Raman spectra of the BiVO4/FeVO4 heterogeneous composites prepared with different molar ratios.

4.4.7 Photocatalytic activity

To determine the photocatalytic activeness of FeVO$_4$, BiVO$_4$ and BiVO$_4$/FeVO$_4$nanophotocatalyst, the degradation rates of crystal violet (CV) model dye were inquired (investigated) in water under visibleradiation from 400 < λ< 800nm. The photocatalytic response of the BiVO$_4$/FeVO$_4$ compound photocatalysts indicated in Fig.4.4.7. It is noticed that the photocatalytic action of

BiVO$_4$/FeVO$_4$ (2:1) is significantly higher to the other samples. It degraded 99.1% of CV dye within 60 min below visible radiation illumination. It is clear that in both cases either we increase FeVO$_4$ mole or BiVO$_4$ mole ratio the photocatalytic activity reduced, however in case of higher concentration of FeVO$_4$ the photocatalytic activity first increases than reduces.

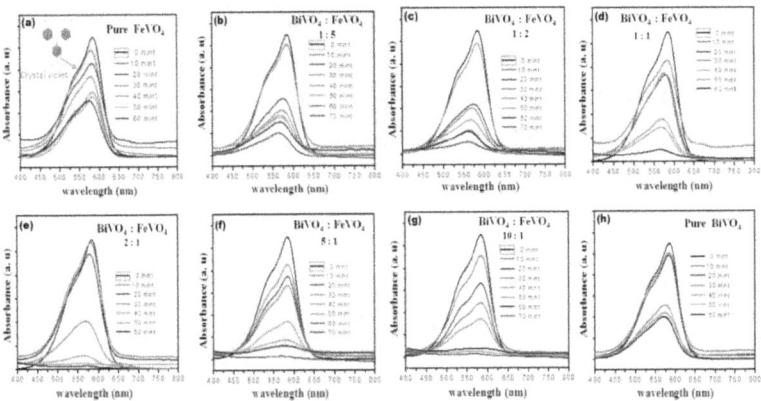

Figure 4.4.7: The photocatalytic degradation of Crystal violet dye by FeVO$_4$, BiVO$_4$ and BiVO$_4$/FeVO$_4$ hetrojunction nanophotocatalyst at **(a)** Pure FeVO$_4$, **(b)** 1:5, **(c)** 1:2, **(d)** 1:1, **(e)** 2:1, **(f)** 5:1, **(g)** 10:1 mole ratio and **(h)** Pure BiVO$_4$.

When the mole ratio is of BiVO$_4$/FeVO$_4$ is (1:5) the photocatalytic degradation efficiency of CV is 71% in 60 min. It perhaps that the appropriate mole ratio of bismuth vanadate and ferric vanadate clouded to form nanocomposite heterojunction BiVO$_4$/FeVO$_4$ photocatalyst is 2:1. The BiVO$_4$/FeVO$_4$ (2:1) heterojunction photocatalysts may facilitate effective electron-hole separation, reduces the recombination rate charges and enhance the absorption of visible light. According to above result and discussion, it is found that at higher concentration of BiVO$_4$ or FeVO$_4$ could lead to reduced photocatalytic activity may be attributed due to some particle of BiVO$_4$ or FeVO$_4$ cannot efficaciously institute composite photocatalyst. In this study BiVO$_4$/FeVO$_4$ (2:1) composite performed higher degradation efficiency and is found the optimal ratio.

The degradation efficiency is determined by using equation 4.2;

$$\text{Degradation Efficiency \%} = (C_o - C_t)/C_o \tag{4.2}$$

Where, C_o is the initial concentration at the time to, and C_t is the concentration at any time t. Figure 4.4.7(a, b) indicate the degradation efficiency at the same dose of the catalyst. The determination of Energy band gap is an important parameter in semiconductor materials for evaluating their properties and applications, so UV-visible spectra of the prepared $BiVO_4/FeVO_4$ nanocomposite was calculated using Tauc plot relation (Brack et al., 2015) as below;

$$(\alpha h\nu) = A(h\nu - E_g)^n \qquad (4.12)$$

Fig. 4.4.7(c) shows E_g value derived out to be 1.9 eV for the $BiVO_4/FeVO_4$ which is in closely matched with the described values.

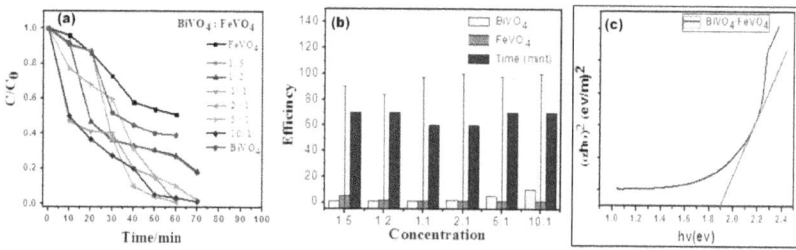

Figure 4.4.8: (a) Concentration changes of CV dye as a function of irradiation time using FeVO4, BiVO4 and BiVO4/FeVO4 at molar ratios of 1 : 5, 1 : 2, 1 : 1, 2 : 1, 5 : 1 and 10 : 1. (b) Degradation error bar profile of CV over BiVO4/FeVO4 at different molar ratios as a function of time. (c) Tauc plot for BiVO4/FeVO4 composite with a 2: 1 ratio.

The photocatalytic mechanism for degradation of CV dye solution by $BiVO_4/FeVO_4$ applied as a nanocatalyst in visible light is illustrated in figure 4.4.8 and can be represented by following equations;

$$BiVO_4/FeVO_4 + h\nu \longrightarrow e^- + h^+ + BiVO_4/FeVO_4 \qquad (4.13)$$

Oxidation occurs at $FeVO_4$ surface

$$h^+ + H_2O \longrightarrow {}^{\bullet}OH + H^+ \qquad (4.14)$$

$$2h^+ + 2H_2O \longrightarrow 2H^+ + H_2O_2 \qquad (4.15)$$

The reduction reaction occurs at $BiVO_4$

$$e^- + O_2 \longrightarrow {}^{\bullet}O_2^- \qquad (4.16)$$

When the visible light is falling on the solution containing crystal violet dye and $BiVO_4/FeVO_4$ photocatalyst, the electron fast move from $FeVO_4$ to $BiVO_4$ while hole of $BiVO_4$ move to the valance band (VB) of $FeVO_4$ and oxidation reaction occurs at VB of $FeVO_4$ where positive holes react with water and formed hydroxyl radical ($^•OH$) radical; while oxidation reaction occurs at conduction band (CB) of $BiVO_4$, where negative electron e^- produces superoxide radical ($^•O_2$) by reacting dissolved oxygen. The superoxide radical and hydroxide radical from both ends oxidize the toxic dye $C_{25}H_{30}ClN_3$ molecule and decompose it into harmless or non-toxic molecules with CO_2, H_2O, and NO_3 byproducts as equation 4.17 indicate below. During this process various primary active species indicating a photogenerated hole, singlet oxygen, hydroxyl radical and superoxide radicals could be created during the Uv-visible degradation process (Lee et al., 2015; Lin et al., 2016; C.-T. Yang et al., 2016). According to the previous study, in the presence of N_2 and radical scavenger suggested $^•OH$ and $^•O_2^-$ are two main active species in the entire process (Chou, Chen, et al., 2016; Jiang et al., 2015; Lee et al., 2015; Lee et al., 2017; F.-Y. Liu, Y.-R. Jiang, et al., 2018; F.-Y. Liu, J.-H. Lin, et al., 2018a; Siao et al., 2018; C.-T. Yang et al., 2016). From previous resultsthe dominant active oxygen species generated in direct oxidation and photocatalytic reactions were $^1O_2$ and $^•OH$ radical (Chen et al., 2017; Chou, Chung, et al., 2016; Huang et al., 2014; Lee et al., 2015). On the basis of the abovestudy and results the probability of forming $^°OH$ should be much lower than that for $^°O_2$, yet, hydroxyl radical is an extremely strong oxidizing agent, which takes the degradation process to either partial or complete mineralization of various organic contaminations.

$$C_{25}H_{30}ClN_3 + (^•OH, ^•O_2-) \longrightarrow CO_2 + H_2O + NO_3 + \text{Other-intermediate} \quad (4.17)$$

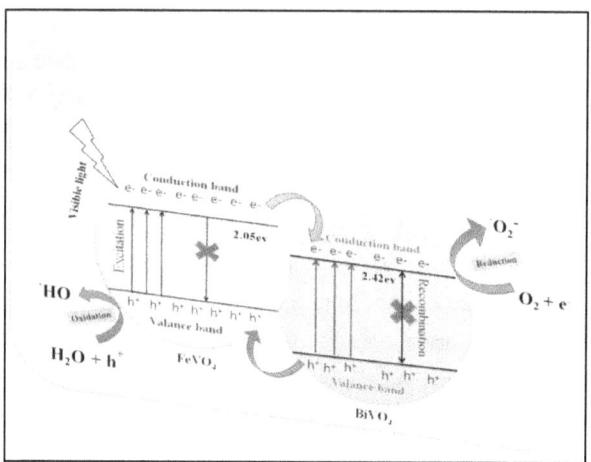

Figure 4.4.9: Reaction mechanism of crystal violet photodegradation over BiVO$_4$/FeVO$_4$ composite under the visible light.

On the basis of the aforementioned literature study, (Chen et al., 2017; Chou, Chung, et al., 2016; Jiang et al., 2015; F.-Y. Liu, J.-H. Lin, et al., 2018a; C.-T. Yang et al., 2016) once the electron entered the conduction band of BiVO4, it induces oxygen, which causes for decomposition of CV dye. Hydroxyl radicals were also produced by the reaction of O°$_2$ radicals with H$^+$ ions and h+ holes with OH$^-$ ions or H$_2$O. no electron paramagnetic resonance (EPR) signal was noticed as the reaction was executed in the dark, whereas the signals with intensities corresponding to the characteristic peaks of DMPO-OH° and DMPO-O°$_2$ adducts were observed during the reaction process in EPR experiment, in figure 4.4.10, not only the six characteristic peaks of the DMPO–O$_2^{-\bullet}$ observed, in addition the four characteristic peaks of DMPO–°OH radical (1 : 2 : 2 : 1 quartet pattern) was also observed by irradiation BiVO$_4$/FeVO$_4$ heterojunction nanocomposite solution under visible light. The decay of CV dye by the generated oxidant species can be squeeze out by equation (4.18 and 19).

$$CV + O_2^{\cdot -} \quad\quad\quad \text{decomposed compounds (4.18)}$$

$$CV + OH^{\cdot} \quad\quad\quad \text{decomposed compounds (4.19)}$$

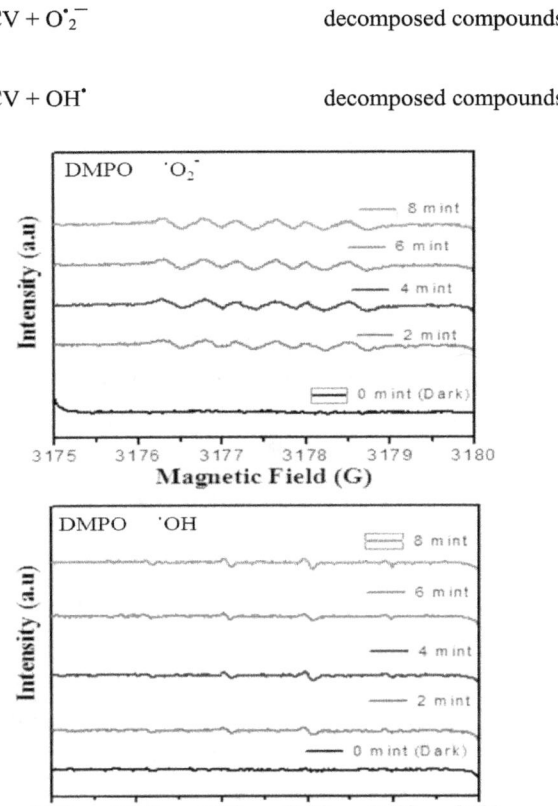

Figure 4.4.10: DMPO spin trapping EPR spectra for DMPO- $O_2^{\cdot -}$ and DMPO-$^{\cdot}OH^{-}$ in visible light irradiation with BiVO$_4$/FeVO$_4$ photocatalyst.

The effect of catalyst dose, dye concentration, stability and recyclability factors were also investigated as are given in figure 4.4.10. The absorption spectra of CV solution using the BiVO$_4$/FeVO$_4$ with different dose at 0, 2.5, and 5 mg/10mL, it is observed that rate of degradation decreases as the dose of the BiVO4/FeVO4 decreasing by 5 mg/10 mL to 0 mg/10 mL in CV solutions. This implies that the amount of BiVO4/FeVO4 catalyst has a significant effect in the photocatalytic reaction for the decomposition of CV organic dyes. Dye concentration effect was evaluated by taking a different initial concentration of CV dye (10-50 mgL^{-1}) and the result are shown in figure 4.4.10(b). The colour removal efficiency decreases as the CV concentration is increased; this is due to the fact that increasing concentration of CV prevents light penetration into the solution. Secondly the number of CV molecule absorbed on the catalyst surface is increased while the number of OH and O radical remain the same under specific conditions. Furthermore, the stability and recyclability of the BiVO4/FeVO4 heterogeneous photocatalyst were also investigated as shown in figure 4.4.11(b). The photocatalytic activity was evaluated three times with the BiVO$_4$/FeVO$_4$ photocatalyst and the sample showed superb stability as well as recyclability.

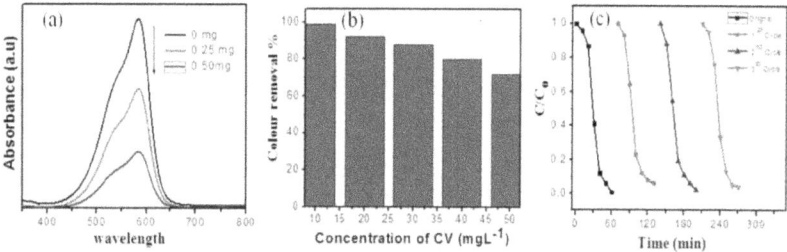

Figure 4.4.11: **(a)** Absorption spectra of CV solution at different concentration of BiVO$_4$/FeVO$_4$ in 10mL CV solution, for 1h respectively. **(b)**Effect of the initial dye concentration on photocatalytic degradation of CV **(c)**Stability curves of the BiVO$_4$/FeVO$_4$ photocatalyst for CV dye under visible light.

4.4.8 Photoluminescence (PL)

The photoluminescence spectra exhibit the recombination rate and electron-hole separation within the photocatalysts. The higher PL intensity shows higher the electron-hole recombination order, which reduces the photocatalytic degradation efficiency(Arshad et al., 2017). The lower the PL peak intensity indicating reduced recombination which results in efficient charge transfer over the catalyst surface in semiconductor (Fatima et al., 2017; Shifu et al., 2009). So the low recombination allows superior dye degradation that is consistent with the photocatalytic results as shown in figure 4.4.12.

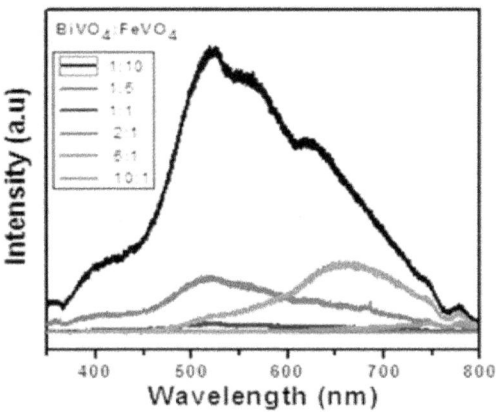

Figure 4.4.12: PL spectra of the BiVO$_4$/FeVO$_4$ composites at different concentrations.

4.4.9 Electrochemical Impedance spectroscopy (EIS)

Electrochemical Impedance spectroscopy is a versatile tool for analysis of conductivity, surface analysis, and electron transfer (Lizhai Pei et al., 2015). It was noticed that in all electrolytes the impedance spectrum is either semicircle or nearly circle at higher ac frequency and a line at low modulation ac frequency as shown in figure 4.4.13. Moreover, in the modified BiVO$_4$/FeVO$_4$ nanocomposite GCE the diameter of the Nyquist circle decreases as compared to bare GCE, indicating that BiVO$_4$/FeVO$_4$ nanocomposite has much higher electron transfer on the surface and superior electrochemical activity, as a result, the resistance decreases and improve the electron transfer process. Cyclic voltammetry was used for detection ascorbic acid analyte for BiVO$_4$/FeVO$_4$ nanocomposite material.

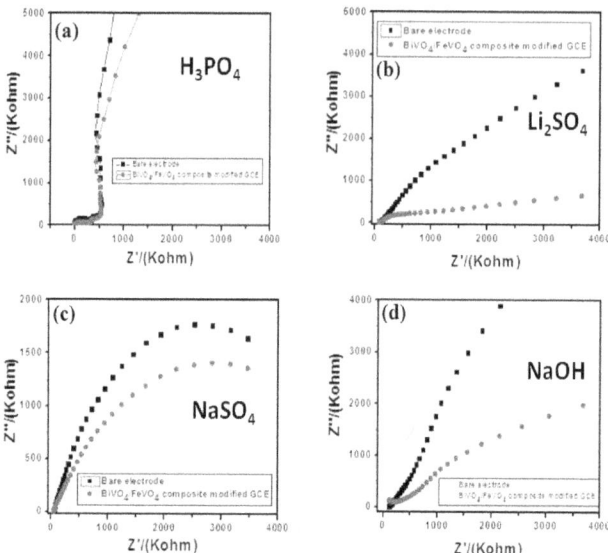

Figure 4.4.13: Electrochemical Impedance spectroscopy of bare and modified BiVO4/FeVO4 nanocomposite GCE in different electrolytes **(a)** 0.1 M H3PO4, **(b)** 0.1 M Li2SO4, **(c)** 0.1 M NaSO4 and **(d)** 0.1 M of NaOH.

Cyclic voltammetry displayed the reaction of bare electrode and modified GC electrode both in presence and absence of 0.5 mM AA at a scan rate 50 mvs^{-1} at -1 to 1 Vs^{-1} as shown in Figure 4.4.14 (a). Bare electrode and modified glassy carbon electrode in H$_3$PO$_4$ solution did not show any oxidation peak both in the absence and presence A.A. molecule; however, the enhanced current was observed which shows that semiconductor material has potential to change the current intensity. In LiSO$_4$ solution (Fig. 4.4.14b) Bare GCE gives one oxidation and one reduction peaks located at 0.20 V and -0.20 V respectively. While the BiVO$_4$/FeVO$_4$ nanocomposite GCE response showed two anodic peaks (cvp1= -0.36 V, cvp2 = -0.17 V) and two cathode peaks (cvp1'= 0.52 V, cvp2' = 0.19 V) as well as increasing the current intensity. In case of NaSO4 solution (Fig. 4.4.14c) the bare electrode did not show any oxidation and reduction but modified BiVO4/FeVO4 nanocomposite GCE show two anodic peaks (cvp1= -0.49 V, cvp2 = -0.71 V). In case of base solution NaOH the bare GCE did not give any response as shown in (Fig. 4.4.14d) however modified BiVO₄/FeVO₄ nanocomposite GCE show change in current intensity as well as one reduction peak (cvp= -0.05 V) and one oxidation peak located at (cvṕ = -0.59 V).

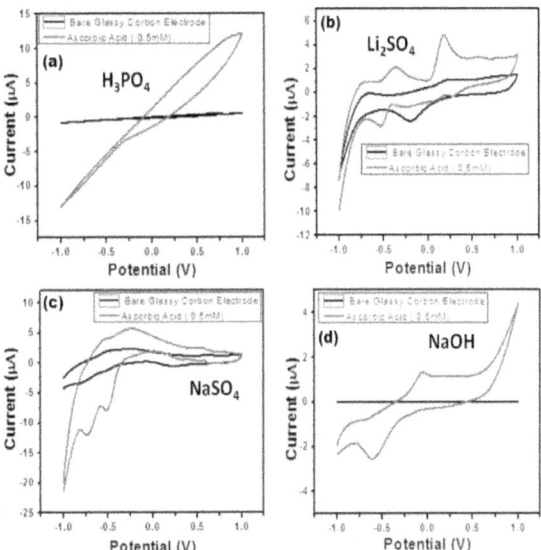

Figure 4.4.14: CVs of the BiVO4/FeVO4 modified GCE in **(a)** 0.1 M H₃PO₄, **(b)** 0.1 M Li₂SO₄, **(c)** 0.1 M NaSO₄ and **(d)** 0.1 M of NaOH solution in the absence and presence of 0.5 mM ascorbic acid, Scan rate 50 mVs⁻¹.

For long-term stability confirmation we stored modified BiVO₄/FeVO₄ nanocomposite GCE for one month at room temperature and used for sensing ascorbic acid it was found that it detects A.A. without any decrease in current, furthermore we checked its reproducibility after twenty measurements it gives little bit relative slandered deviation from the original value, as indicated in figure 4.4.15. So the modified BiVO₄/FeVO₄ nanocomposite GCE comprises noble stability and reproducibility for A.A. electrochemical determination.

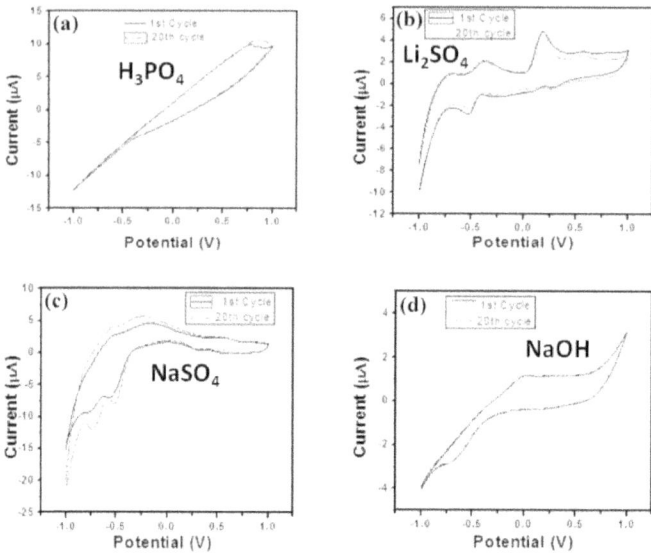

Figure 4.4.15: CVs of the BiVO4/FeVO4 modified GCE in mixed **(a)** 0.1 M H$_3$PO$_4$, **(b)** 0.1 M Li$_2$SO$_4$, **(c)** 0.1 M NaSO$_4$, **(d)** 0.1 M of NaOH and Ascorbic acid (0.5mM) solution Scan rate 50 mVs^{-1}, recycling for 1st and 20th time.

Section-V

4.5 Preparation and characterizations of $Zn_3(VO_4)_2/BiVO_4$ composite for the photocatalytic degradation of methylene blue organic dye and detection of H_2O_2

4.5.1 Introduction

In this work, a $Zn_3(VO_4)_2/BiVO_4$ heterojunction nanocomposite photocatalyst has been prepared using the hydrothermal route with different molar concentration ratio. The as-synthesized nano photocatalyst was characterized using XRD, SEM, EDS, XPS, FT-IR, Raman, BET, UV-Vis DRS, EPR and PL. The effect of molar ratio on composition and morphology was studied. The prepared nano-composite exhibited excellent photocatalytic response by completely degrading the model pollutant methylene blue (MB) dye in 60 minutes at molar concentration ratio 2:1. In the basic medium at pH of 12 the $Zn_3(VO_4)_2/BiVO_4$ nanocomposite degrades MB completely within 45 mint. The nanocomposite was also successfully used for the electrochemical detection of an important analyte hydrogen peroxide (H_2O_2). This study opens up a new horizon for the potential applications of $Zn_3(VO_4)_2/BiVO_4$ nanocomposite in environmental wastewater remediation as well as in biosensing sciences.

4.5.2 X-Rays Diffraction (XRD)

Fig. 4.5.1 shows the XRD diffraction pattern of as-synthesised $Zn_3(VO_4)_2/BiVO_4$, at variant concentration ratio for phase structures. The XRD diffraction peaks of $Zn_3(VO_4)_2/BiVO_4$ together belong to pure Zn3 (VO4)2 (JCPD card 19-1468) and to $BiVO_4$ (JCPD card 75-1867) hence the pattern of $Zn_3(VO_4)_2/BiVO_4$ heterojunction photocatalyst compound exhibited characteristic diffraction peaks from both $BiVO_4$ and $Zn_3(VO_4)_2$ crystalline phases, which verifying that $Zn_3(VO_4)_2/BiVO_4$ composite synthesised with success by facile hydrothermal route at varied mole ratio. It can be seen as the BiVO4 ratios increases the $Zn_3(VO_4)_2$ peaks diminish due to the brooding of $BiVO_4$ peaks.

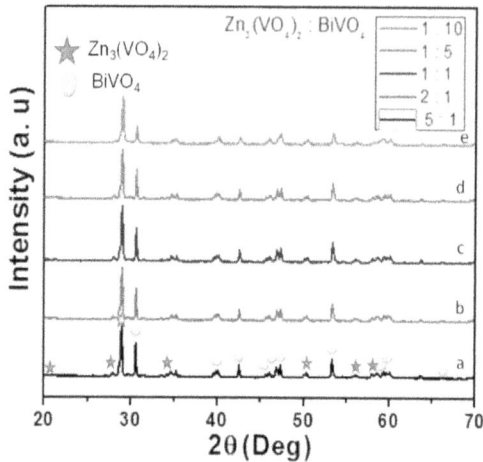

Figure 4.5.1: XRD spectrum of $Zn_3(VO_4)_2/BiVO_4$ heterojunction composite at different mole ratio **(a)** 5:1, **(b)** 2:1, **(c)** 1:1, **(d)** 1:5, and **(e)** 1:10

4.5.3 Scanning Electron Microscopy (SEM)

To study morphology, of the as-synthesised $Zn_3(VO_4)_2/BiVO_4$ heterojunction was characterized by FESEM. The $Zn_3(VO_4)_2/BiVO_4$ nanoparticles and nanorods with high yield are observed as shown in Fig. 4.5.2(a-e). It was noticed that as the ratio of $BiVO_4$ increased it develops large particle size, may be due to the aggregation/agglomeration of the particles as it can be seen in Fig. 4.5.2(e). For chemical composition the Energy Dispersive Spectroscopy analysis is performed, it is seen that the main elements within the samples are Vanadium, Zinc, Bismuth, Oxygen at different mole ratios, the carbon and platinum peaks are raised due to carbon tape and Pt. coating.

Figure 4.5.2: SEM images of $Zn_3(VO_4)_2$/$BiVO_4$ composite heterojunction photocatalyst at different mole ratio **(a)** 5:1, **(b)** 2:1, **(c)** 1:1, **(d)** 1:5, **(e)** 1:10 and **(f)** EDS analysis of $Zn_3(VO_4)_2$/$BiVO_4$ composite at mole ratio 1:1.

4.5.4 Photocatalysis

Fig. 4.5.3 showed the changes in the visible (UV-vis) spectra during the photodegradation process of MB dye in aqueous $Zn_3(VO_4)_2$/$BiVO_4$ solution under visible light radiation. It was noticed that at ratio 2:1 of $Zn_3(VO_4)_2$/$BiVO_4$ heterogeneous photocatalyst about whole dye degraded in 90 mint.

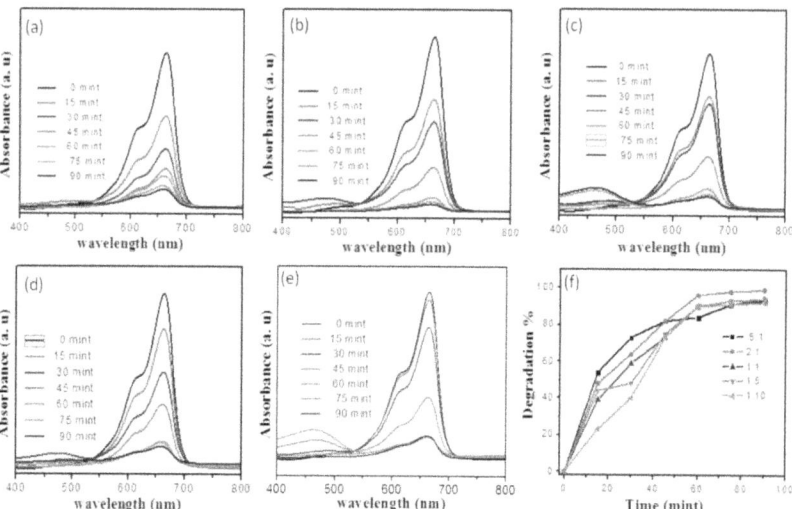

Figure 4.5.3: UV-vis absorption spectra of Methylene blue dye for different irradiation times showing photocatalytic degradation of Methylene blue dye through $Zn_3(VO_4)_2$/$BiVO_4$ heterogeneous nano photocatalyst at mole ratio **(a)** 5:1, **(b)** 2:1, **(c)** 1:1, **(d)** 1:5, **(e)** 1:10 and **(f)** Efficiency of MB dye as a function of irradiation time in the presence of photocatalyst at same quantity but different mole ratios.

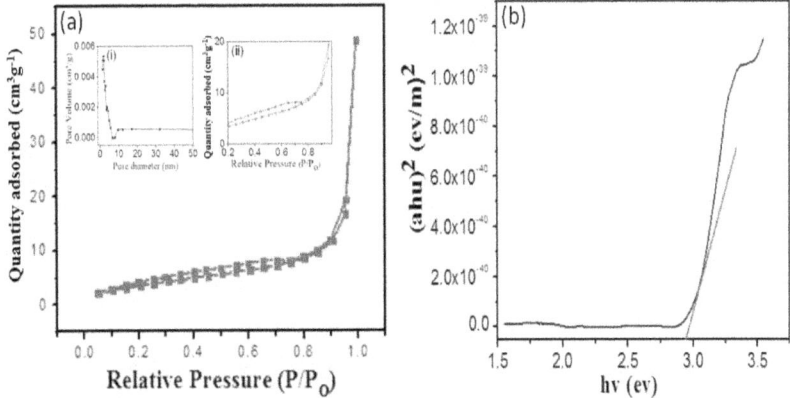

Figure 4.5.4:(a) N2 adsorption–desorption isotherm distribution curves for $Zn_3(VO_4)_2/BiVO_4$ at 2:1 mole ratio, inset (i) differential pore size distribution curve from Barret-Joyner-Halender (BJH) method (ii) high resolution N_2 adsorption–desorption isotherm at 2:1 mole ratio **(b)** Tauc plot for $Zn_3(VO_4)_2/BiVO_4$ composite at 2:1 mole ratio.

The photocatalytic chemical mechanism of MB dye solution by $Zn_3(VO_4)_2/BiVO_4$ nano photocatalyst in visible light can be presented through the following equations;

$Zn_3(VO_4)_2/BiVO_4 + h\nu$ → $e^- + h^+ + Zn_3(VO_4)_2/BiVO_4$ (4.20)

Oxidation occurs at BiVO4 surfaces

$h^+ + H_2O$ → $^\bullet OH + H^+$ (4.21)

$2h^+ + 2H_2O$ → $2H^+ + H_2O_2$ (4.22)

Reduction reaction occurs at $Zn_3(VO_4)_2$

$e^- + O_2$ → $^\bullet O_2^-$ (4.23)

When the visible light is interacting with the Methylene blue dye and $Zn_3(VO_4)_2/BiVO_4$ photocatalyst solution, the electron move from $BiVO_4$ to $Zn_3(VO_4)_2$ while hole of $Zn_3(VO_4)_2$ move to the valence band (V_B) of $BiVO_4$ and oxidation reaction occurs at V_B of $Zn_3(VO_4)_2/BiVO_4$ where positive holes react with water and formed hydroxyl radical ($^\bullet OH$) radical; while reduction occurs at conduction band (C_B) of $BiVO_4$, where negative electron (e^-) produces superoxide radical (•O2) by reacting dissolved oxygen. Pseudo first order equation 4.3 was applied to extract the reaction kinetics of the organic dye;

$$\ln(C/C_o) = -kt \tag{4.3}$$

Where C is the concentration of the dye at a time "t", C_o is the concentration at a time "to" and k is pseudo-first order rate constant. Evaluates of degradation rate constant k for MB over $Zn_3(VO_4)_2/BiVO_4$ under visible light irradiation applying pseudo first order was calculated to be 0.01522, 0.01922, 0.01296, 0.01325 and 0.01076 min−1 respectively at ratios 5:1, 2:1, 1:1, 1:5, and 1:10. It was observed that dye solution with 2:1 value of $Zn_3(VO_4)_2/BiVO_4$ exhibited the highestphotodegradation efficiency as shown in Fig. 4.5.4.

The concentration changes against the irradiation illuminated time and degradation efficiency graph are shown in Fig. 4.5.4. When the light is illuminated over the solution, active species hydroxyl radical, hole, $\bar{O}_2$ and $^{\bullet}O_2$ are generated during the photocatalytic degradation reaction in visible light illumination. The formation of $OH^{\bullet}$ radicals is much lower than $O_2^{\bullet}$, however hydroxyl radical is highly active and non-selective oxidant agent species for degradation which leads to mineralization of organic chemicals. (Chou, Chen, et al., 2016; Chou, Chung, et al., 2016; Lee et al., 2015; F.-Y. Liu, Y.-R. Jiang, et al., 2018; C.-T. Yang et al., 2016; Zeng et al., 2018)

The degradation efficiency is determined by following the equation;

$$\text{Degradation Efficiency \%} = (C_o - C_t)/C_o \tag{4.2}$$

Where, C_o is the initial concentration at the time t_o, and C_t is the concentration at any time t. Fig. 4.5.5(a, b) indicate the degradation efficiency at the same dose as the catalyst.

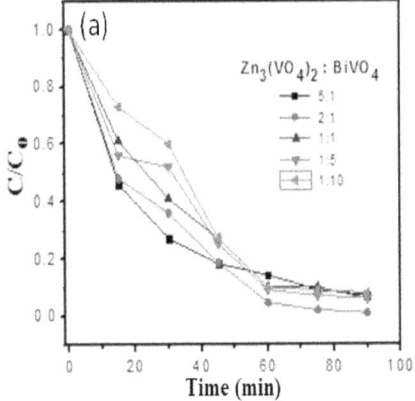
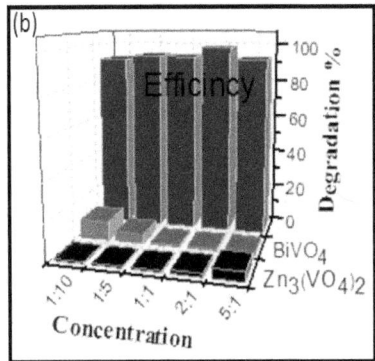

The pH effect was also examined at a different value (2, 5, 7, 10 and 12) as illustrated in Fig. 4.5.6, it is observed that at pH- The 12 the MB aqueous solution was totally degraded in 45 mint, due to the excess amount of OH$^{\bullet}$ radicals, hydroxyl radical is a strong oxidant agent so from one side O$^{\bullet}_2$ degrading and on the other side OH$^{\bullet}$ as a result about totally (99.6 %) degradation was observed within 45 mint. During the Photocatalytic activity degradation process the new absorption the band and peak shift observed could be due to the decomposing of the benzene ring in the dye chain.

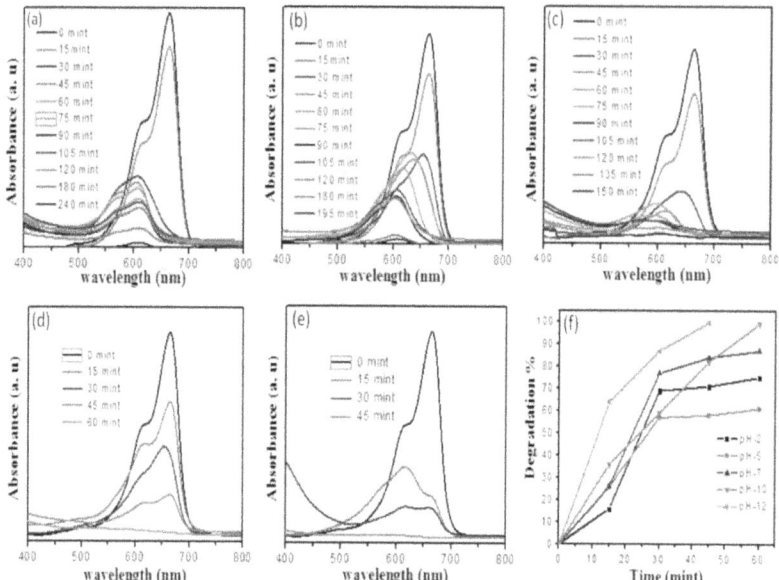

Figure 4.5.6: UV-vis absorption spectra of Methylene blue dye for different irradiation times showing photocatalytic degradation of Methylene blue dye using $Zn_3(VO_4)_2/BiVO_4$ heterogeneous nano photocatalyst at pH **(a)** 2, **(b)** 5, **(c)** 7, **(d)** 10, **(e)** 12, and **(f)** Efficiency of MB dye as a function of irradiation time at different pH values in the presence of photocatalyst.

Concentration changes against the irradiation illuminated time and degradation efficiency graph at various pH values are shown in Fig. 4.5.7.

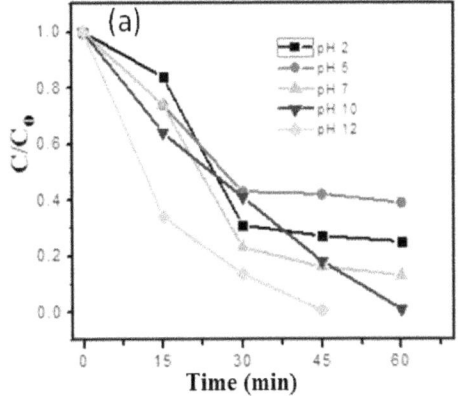
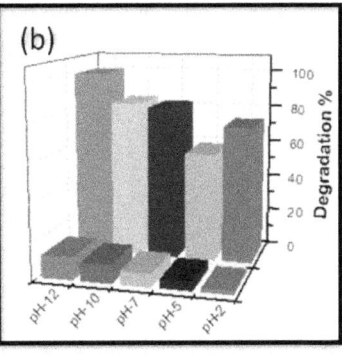

The superoxide radical and hydroxide radical from both ends oxidize the toxic dye $C_{16}H_{18}ClN_3S$ molecule and decompose it into harmless or non-toxic molecules with CO_2, H_2O, NO_2 and benzene byproducts as indicated below.

$$C_{16}H_{18}ClN_3S + (OH^\bullet, {}^\bullet O_2^-) \longrightarrow H_2O + CO_2 + NO_2 + SO_2 + C_6H_6 \quad (4.24)$$

4.5.5 Photoluminescnce (PL)

The photoluminescence (PL) spectrum exposes the recombination rate and charges (electron, hole) separation within the semiconductor nano-photocatalyst. The higher PL intensity indicates that there is a higher rate of recombination which causes lower degradation efficiency. (Arshad et al., 2017; Liu et al., 2016) In PL spectra the lower intensity indicates the reduced and controlled recombination which results in the effectiveelectron-hole transfer over the photocatalyst surface and allows superior degradation of contaminants that increases the photocatalyst efficiency as shown in Fig. 4.5.8(a). (Fatima et al., 2017; Shifu et al., 2009)Moreover, the reusability of $Zn_3(VO_4)_2/BiVO_4$ nano photocatalyst at a ratio (2:1) was also checked as shown in Fig. 4.5.8(b). The photolytic activity was repeated three times and the sample showed good stability.

On the basis of the above-mentioned literature study, once the electron entered the conduction band of $Zn_3(VO_4)_2$, it brings oxygen, which makes bases for decomposition of MB dye. Hydroxyl radicals were also produced by the reaction of $^•O_2$ radicals with H^+ ions and h^+ holes with H_2O. It was noticed, no electron paramagnetic resonance (EPR) signal was found when the reaction was performed in the dark, whereas the signals with intensities corresponding to the characteristic peaks of DMPO–OH$^•$ adducts were observed during the reaction process in the EPR experiment, but no peaks of DMPO-$^•O_2$ were observed as shown in Fig. 4.5.9, the four characteristic peaks of DMPO–OH$^•$ radical (1: 2: 2: 1 quartet pattern) was observed by irradiation $Zn_3(VO_4)_2/BiVO_4$ heterojunction nanocomposite solution under visible light. The decay of MB dye by the generated oxidant species can be squeezed out by the following equation.

$$MB + OH^• \quad\quad\quad \text{decomposed compounds} \quad\quad\quad (4.25)$$

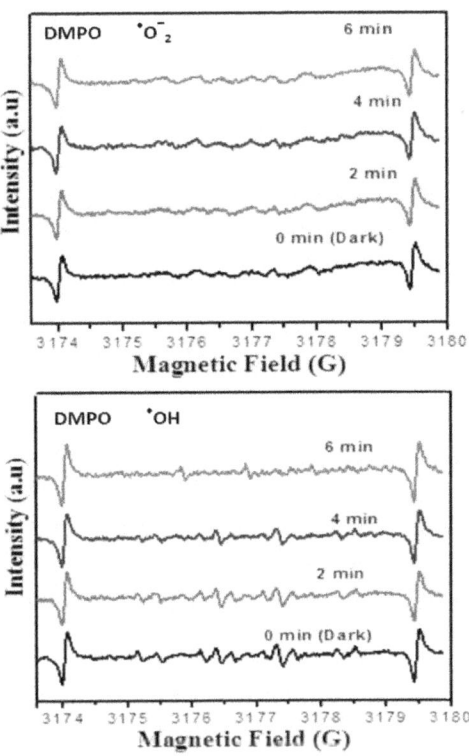

Figure 4.5.9: DMPO spin trapping EPR spectra for DMPO–$^{•}O_2^-$ and DMPO–$^{•}OH^-$ in visible light irradiation with $Zn_3(VO_4)_2/BiVO_4$ photocatalyst.

Here, Comparison of Photocatalytic activity of some previous reported photocatalysts and present $Zn_3(VO_4)_2/BiVO_4$ for degradation of Methylene blue dye under visible light irradiation is given in table 4.5.

Table 4.5. The degradation comparison of Methylene blue dye using the $Zn_3(VO_4)_2/BiVO_4$ composite with other nanomaterial photocatalysts.

Catalyst	Efficiency%	Light source	Time (mint)	Reference
ZnS	88	Visible light	90	(Rao et al., 2016)
V_2O_3/CNT/TiO_2	70	Visible light	120	(Chen et al., 2010)
$BiVO_4$/ TiO_2	86	Visible light	120	(Pingmuang et al., 2016)
CuO-$BiVO_4$	92	Visible light	300	(Abdullah et al., 2016)
P-25, Degussa	89	Visible light	120	(Li et al., 2017)
$Zn_3(VO_4)_2/BiVO_4$	98.91	Visible light	90	Present work
$Zn_3(VO_4)_2/BiVO_4$ at pH-12	99.6	Visible light	45	Present work

4.5.6 Electrochemical Impedance Spectroscopy (EIS)

Electrochemical Impedance Spectroscopy (EIS) Nyquist Plots analysis represents a flexible tool for conductivity analysis, surface psychoanalysis, and electrons transmit. (Lizhai Pei et al., 2015) From Fig. 4.5.10 it is clear that impedance spectrum is either semicircle or nearly circle at higher ac frequency and a line at low modulation ac frequency. The Nyquist circle diameter of $Zn_3(VO_4)_2/BiVO_4$ is much lower than bare Glassy Carbon electrode, indicating that the electron transfer in $Zn_3(VO_4)_2/BiVO_4$ composite is much sharper than the bare GCE and resulting decrease in resistance.

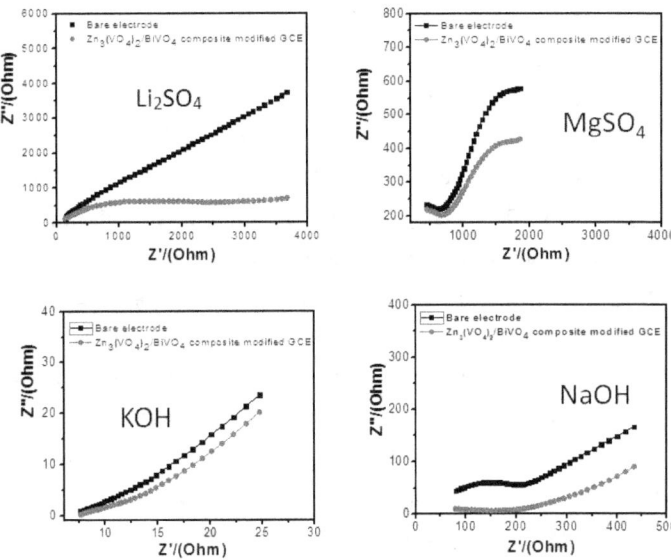

Figure 4.5.10: Electrochemical Impedance spectroscopy of bare and modified $Zn_3(VO_4)_2/BiVO_4$ nanocomposite GCE in different electrolytes **(a)** 0.1 M Li_2SO_4, **(b)** 0.1 M $MgSO_4$, **(c)** 0.1 M KOH and **(d)** 0.1 M of NaOH.

Hydrogen peroxide or H_2O_2 is pale-blue liquid and exists among the most important analyte. H_2O_2 is used in several areas, for food processes, environmental analysis, fabric manufacture, pharmaceutical, medical diagnostics, clinical laboratory, antiseptic and disinfecting agents, powerful oxidizing agents and are also involved in several biological events as a by-product of oxidases. Higher concentration of H_2O_2 (>50 µM) can cause stomach irritation, tissue burns, on the other hand, low levels of H_2O_2 effects on the physiology of human fibroblasts; so to develop an accurate, sensitive, highly reliable as well as low cost sensitizer for hydrogen peroxide (H_2O_2) is the demand of time. In this scenario, electrochemical sensors with fast response, superior selectivity and high sensitivity, easy to operate and low cost is the optimal option for actualizing the accurate detection of Hydrogen peroxide. (Min Liu et al., 2017; Yu et al., 2017; Zeki Bas et al., 2017) Cyclic voltammetry was exploited for measurement and detection of Hydrogen peroxide analyte for $Zn_3(VO_4)_2/BiVO_4$ nanocomposite material. Cyclic voltammetry showed the response of bare electrode and glassy carbon modified electrode both in presence and absence of 0.5mM Hydrogen peroxide at a scan rate of -1 to 1 Vs^{-1} as shown in Fig. 4.5.11(a).

In Li_2SO_4 solution (Fig. 4.5.11a) bare GCE gives one oxidation and one reduction peaks located at 0.18 V and -0.43 V, while the modified $Zn_3(VO_4)_2/BiVO_4$ glassy carbon electrode gives enhanced current and CV voltammogram with one oxidation and one reduction peaks located at 0.07 V and -0.37 V respectively. In $MgSO_4$ bare electrode and modified glassy carbon electrode solution did not show any oxidation peak both in the absence and presence H_2O_2; however, the enhanced current was observed which shows that semiconductor material has potential to change the current intensity (Fig. 4.5.11b). In KOH solution (Fig. 4.5.11c) again no oxidation or reduction peak was observed for both bare GCE and modified $Zn_3(VO_4)_2/BiVO_4$ nanocomposite GCE, however, showed enhanced current intensity in case of modified nanocomposite GCE indicating the potential for changing the current. In case of NaOH solution (Fig. 4.5.11d) the bare electrode shows one oxidation and reduction peak at 0.15 and -0.5, while the modified $Zn_3(VO_4)_2/BiVO_4$ nanocomposite GCE show change in enhanced current intensity as well as one oxidation and reduction peak at 0.049 and -0.34 V respectively. From the above-detailed CV spectra, the outputs showing the formation of $Zn_3(VO_4)2/BiVO_4$ as the sensor was evidenced.

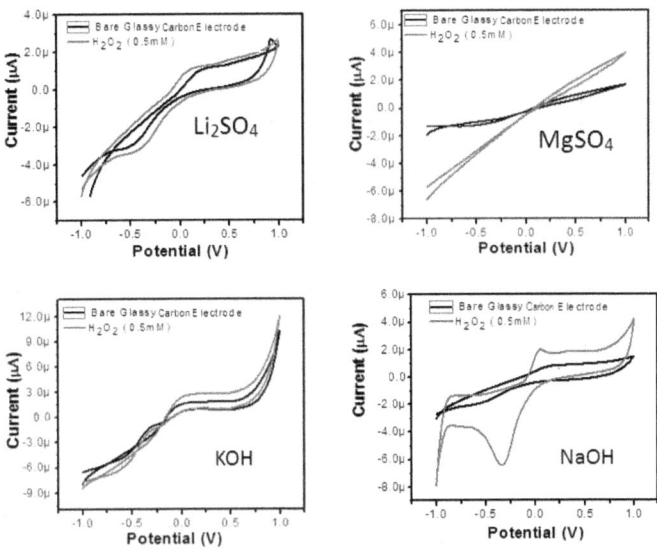

Figure 4.5.11: CVs of the $Zn_3(VO_4)_2/BiVO_4$ modified GCE in **(a)** 0.1 M Li_2SO_4, **(b)** 0.1 M $MgSO_4$, **(c)** 0.1 M of KOH and **(d)** 0.1 M of NaOH solution in the absence and presence of 0.5 mM Hydrogen peroxide at scan rate: 50 mV s^{-1}.

For long-term stability confirmation we stored modified $Zn_3(VO_4)_2/BiVO_4$ composite GCE for three weeks at ambient temperature and used for sensing H_2O_2 it was found that modified $Zn_3(VO_4)_2/BiVO_4$ showed detection of H_2O_2 although there is decrease in current from the first day values but its retain reproducibility after twenty measurements it gives little relative standard deviation from the original value, as shown in Fig. 4.5.12. So the modified $Zn_3(VO_4)_2/BiVO_4$ composite GCE show stability and reproducibility for H_2O_2 electrochemical determination.

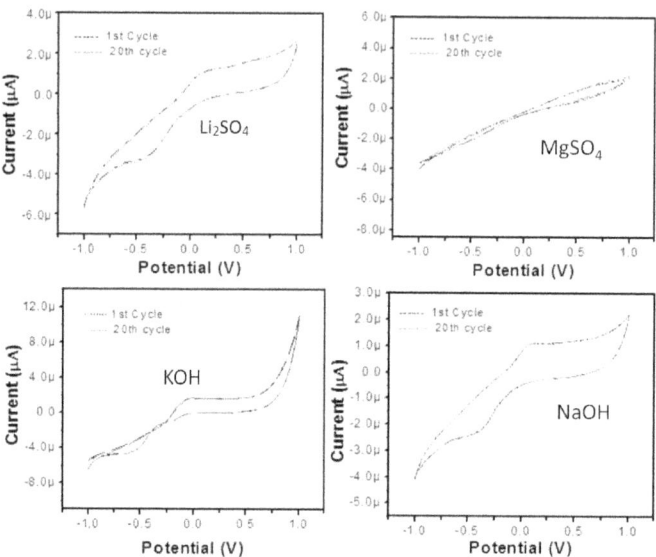

Figure 4.5.12: CVs of the $Zn_3(VO_4)_2/BiVO_4$ modified GCE in mixed **(a)** 0.1 M LiSO4 **(b)** 0.1 M MgSO4, **(c)** 0.1 M KOH, **(d)** 0.1 M of NaOH and Hydrogen peroxide (0.5mM) solution Scan rate: 50 mV s^{-1}, recycling for 1st and 20th time.

CHAPTER 5
SUMMARY

In this study, we explored the potential of hydrothermally grown $BiVO_4$, $FeVO_4$, $Zn_3(VO_4)_2$, $BiVO_4/FeVO_4$ and $Zn_3(VO_4)_2/BiVO_4$ nanostructures for the photocatalytic decomposition of organic dyes as well as for the electrochemical bio-sensing. The prepared nanomaterials were characterized by using powered X-ray diffraction (XRD), Scanning Electron Microscopy (SEM), Energy Dispersive X-ray Spectroscopy (EDX), X-ray photoelectron spectroscopy (XPS), Brunauer–Emmett–Teller (BET), Fourier transform infrared (FTIR), Raman, Photoluminescence (PL) and electron paramagnetic resonance (EPR). The potential of nanomaterials was checked by evaluating photocatalytic decomposition of organic pollutants, pigments and industrial effluents, the electrochemical response has also been checked using Cyclic voltammetry (CV) and electrochemical induce spectroscopy (EIS) techniques. Initially, we prepared template free novel monoclinic Bismuth vanadate (m-$BiVO_4$) nanoparticles, with highly dispersive nature and uniform size of 20-30nm for efficient visible light photocatalytic degradation of organic toxic dyes Rhodamine-B and Crystal violet. The surface area of the as-synthesized nanoparticles was found to be 24.946m^2/g and pore diameter 1.932nm; $BiVO_4$ nanoparticles showed enhance photocatalytic response for the degradation for both dyes under visible light. PL study indicated the ability of the m-$BiVO_4$ nanoparticles for photocatalytic degradation. In the second step, $FeVO_4$ nanoparticles were successfully prepared by facile hydrothermal technique. The $FeVO_4$ nanoparticles exhibited superior photocatalytic activity on Methylene blue (MB) and industrial effluents under visible light irradiation. $FeVO_4$ nanoparticles exhibited significantly large surface area 89.220 m^2g^{-1}, UV-visible analysis confirmed that $FeVO_4$ have a band gap of 2.73eV, indicating the strong affinity to absorption of light in the visible region. These $FeVO_4$ nanoparticles also showed good recyclability as well as stability when it was recycled thrice for degradation of MB dye solution. PL results showed that $FeVO_4$ nanoparticles have a potential in the green visible range. In the third step, we prepared $Zn_3(VO_4)_2$ nanoplates using the simple hydrothermal method. The $Zn_3(VO_4)_2$ nanoplates showed good photocatalytic degradation performance on Congo red and Crystal violet dyes under visible light irradiation. The $Zn_3(VO_4)_2$ have large BET surface area 84 m^2/g, average pore size 9 nm and hysteresis loop of the H_3 type which is associated with groups of plate-like particles giving lamellar pore structure shows the presence of mesopores in the structure. The PL measurement revealed the potential for blue/green visible optical devices. In next step, we fabricate a $BiVO_4/FeVO_4$ nanocomposite by autoclave hydrothermal method using Bismuth nitrate dehydrate $(Bi(NO_3)_3 \cdot 5H_2O)$, Iron nitrate dehydrate $(Fe(NO_3)_3 \cdot 9H_2O)$ as Bismuth and Ferric ion source and Ammonia metavanadate NH_4VO_3 as Vanadium ion source, at different $BiVO_4$ and $FeVO_4$ mole ratio. $BiVO_4/FeVO_4$ nanocomposites were investigated for their activity as nanophotocatalyst by photocatalytic degradation of crystal violet (CV) dye under the visible light irradiation. The $BiVO_4/FeVO_4$ at mole ratio of 2:1 performed superior degradation efficiency owed to higher specific surface area 70.147 cm^2g^{-1} and pore size 3.798nm comprises porosity. The $BiVO_4/FeVO_4$ was studied for electrochemical detection of A.A and it showed good results. Finally, we prepared A $Zn_3(VO_4)_2/BiVO_4$ heterogeneous nano photocatalyst through hydrothermal method, using Bismuth nitrate dehydrate $(Bi(NO_3)_3 \cdot 5H_2O)$, Zinc acetate dehydrate $Zn(O_2CCH_3)_2$ as Bismuth, Zinc ion source and ammonia metavanadate (NH_4VO_3) as Vanadium ion source. $Zn_3(VO_4)_2/BiVO_4$ nanocomposites were investigated for the activity of nano photocatalyst by photocatalytic degradation of Methylene blue (MB) toxic dye in the visible light radiation. It exhibited exceptional outcome and decompose the toxic dye into mineral products in 45 mints at pH-12. The $Zn_3(VO_4)_2/BiVO_4$ nanocomposites was also examined for electrochemical detection of an important analyte Hydrogen peroxide (H_2O_2) and it showed good results. Thus, this work indicates the potential of $BiVO_4$, $FeVO_4$, $Zn_3(VO_4)_2$, $BiVO_4/FeVO_4$ and $Zn_3(VO_4)_2/BiVO_4$ nanomaterials for multifaceted applications, as environmental remediation and bio sensing. It gives direction for designing more efficient photocatalysts in future for treating dye effluents, industrial wastewater and sensor applications.

References

Abdullah, A. H., Peng, W. T., & Hussein, M. Z. (2016). Degradation of methylene blue dye by CuO-BiVO4 photocatalysts under visible light irradiation. *Malaysian Journal of Analytical Sciences, 20*(6), 1338-1345.

Adhikari, S., Gupta, R., Surin, A., Kumar, T. S., Chakraborty, S., Sarkar, D., & Madras, G. (2016). Visible light assisted improved photocatalytic activity of combustion synthesized spongy-ZnO towards dye degradation and bacterial inactivation. *RSC Advances, 6*(83), 80086-80098.

Ahmad, M., Pan, C., & Zhu, J. (2010). Investigation of hydrogen storage capabilities of ZnO-based nanostructures. *The Journal of Physical Chemistry C, 114*(6), 2560-2565.

Ahmed, S., Rasul, M., Brown, R., & Hashib, M. (2011). Influence of parameters on the heterogeneous photocatalytic degradation of pesticides and phenolic contaminants in wastewater: a short review. *Journal of environmental management, 92*(3), 311-330.

Ahmed, T., Zhang, H.-l., Gao, Y.-Y., Xu, H.-b., & Zhang, Y. (2018). Surfactant-free synthesis of m-BiVO4 nanoribbons and enhanced visible-light photocatalytic properties. *Materials Research Bulletin, 99*, 298-305.

Ahmed, T., Zhang, H.-l., Xu, H.-b., & Zhang, Y. (2017). m-BiVO4 hollow spheres coated on carbon fiber with superior reusability as photocatalyst. *Colloids and Surfaces A: Physicochemical and Engineering Aspects, 531*, 213-220.

Alagiri, M., Ponnusamy, S., & Muthamizhchelvan, C. (2012). Synthesis and characterization of NiO nanoparticles by sol–gel method. *Journal of Materials Science: Materials in Electronics, 23*(3), 728-732.

Ali, A., & Oh, W.-C. (2017). Preparation of Ag 2 Se-Graphene-TiO 2 Nanocomposite and its Photocatalytic Degradation (Rh B). *Journal of the Korean Ceramic Society, 54*(5), 388-394.

Anku, W., Oppong, S. O.-B., Shukla, S. K., & Govender, P. P. (2016). Comparative photocatalytic degradation of monoazo and diazo dyes under simulated visible light using Fe3+/C/S doped-TiO2 nanoparticles. *Acta Chimica Slovenica, 63*(2), 380-391.

Appavu, B., Thiripuranthagan, S., Ranganathan, S., Erusappan, E., & Kannan, K. (2018). BiVO 4/N-rGO nano composites as highly efficient visible active photocatalyst for the degradation of dyes and antibiotics in eco system. *Ecotoxicology and environmental safety, 151*, 118-126.

Arshad, A., Iqbal, J., Siddiq, M., Mansoor, Q., Ismail, M., Mehmood, F., . . . Abid, Z. (2017). Graphene nanoplatelets induced tailoring in photocatalytic activity and antibacterial characteristics of MgO/graphene nanoplatelets nanocomposites. *Journal of Applied Physics, 121*(2), 024901.

Avansi, W., de Mendonça, V. R., Lopes, O. F., & Ribeiro, C. (2015). Vanadium pentoxide 1-D nanostructures applied to dye removal from aqueous systems by coupling adsorption and visible-light photodegradation. *RSC Advances, 5*(16), 12000-12006.

Bokare, A. D., Chikate, R. C., Rode, C. V., & Paknikar, K. M. (2008). Iron-nickel bimetallic nanoparticles for reductive degradation of azo dye Orange G in aqueous solution. *Applied Catalysis B: Environmental, 79*(3), 270-278.

Boutonnet, M., Kizling, J., Stenius, P., & Maire, G. (1982). The preparation of monodisperse colloidal metal particles from microemulsions. *Colloids and Surfaces, 5*(3), 209-225.

Brack, P., Sagu, J. S., Peiris, T., McInnes, A., Senili, M., Wijayantha, K., . . . Selli, E. (2015). Aerosol-Assisted CVD of Bismuth Vanadate Thin Films and Their Photoelectrochemical Properties. *Chemical Vapor Deposition, 21*(1-2-3), 41-45.

Burcham, L. J., & Wachs, I. E. (1999). The origin of the support effect in supported metal oxide catalysts: in situ infrared and kinetic studies during methanol oxidation. *Catalysis today, 49*(4), 467-484.

Bykov, Y. V., Rybakov, K., & Semenov, V. (2001). High-temperature microwave processing of materials. *Journal of Physics D: Applied Physics, 34*(13), R55.

Chatchai, P., Murakami, Y., Kishioka, S.-y., Nosaka, A. Y., & Nosaka, Y. (2009). Efficient photocatalytic activity of water oxidation over $WO_3/BiVO_4$ composite under visible light irradiation. *Electrochimica Acta, 54*(3), 1147-1152.

Chen, C.-C., Fu, J.-Y., Chang, J.-L., Huang, S.-T., Yeh, T.-W., Hung, J.-T., . . . Chen, L.-W. (2018). Bismuth oxyfluoride/bismuth oxyiodide nanocomposites enhance visible-light-driven photocatalytic activity. *Journal of colloid and interface science, 532*, 375-386.

Chen, C.-C., Yang, C.-T., Chung, W.-H., Chang, J.-L., & Lin, W.-Y. (2017). Synthesis and characterization of $Bi_4Si_3O_{12}$, Bi_2SiO_5, and $Bi_{12}SiO_{20}$ by controlled hydrothermal method and their photocatalytic activity. *Journal of the Taiwan Institute of Chemical Engineers, 78*, 157-167.

Chen, J., Qiu, X., Fang, Z., Yang, M., Pokeung, T., Gu, F., . . . Lan, B. (2012). Removal mechanism of antibiotic metronidazole from aquatic solutions by using nanoscale zero-valent iron particles. *Chemical engineering journal, 181*, 113-119.

Chen, M.-L., & Oh, W.-C. (2010). The improved photocatalytic properties of methylene blue for $V_2O_3/CNT/TiO_2$ composite under visible light. *International Journal of Photoenergy, 2010*.

Chirayil, T., Zavalij, P. Y., & Whittingham, M. S. (1998). Hydrothermal synthesis of vanadium oxides. *Chemistry of Materials, 10*(10), 2629-2640.

Choi, K.-S., & Kim, T. W. (2015). Synthesis of high-surface-area nanoporous bivo4 electrodes: Google Patents.

Chou, S.-Y., Chen, C.-C., Dai, Y.-M., Lin, J.-H., & Lee, W. W. (2016). Novel synthesis of bismuth oxyiodide/graphitic carbon nitride nanocomposites with enhanced visible-light photocatalytic activity. *RSC Advances, 6*(40), 33478-33491.

Chou, S.-Y., Chung, W.-H., Chen, L.-W., Dai, Y.-M., Lin, W.-Y., Lin, J.-H., & Chen, C.-C. (2016). A series of BiO x I y/GO photocatalysts: synthesis, characterization, activity, and mechanism. *RSC Advances, 6*(86), 82743-82758.

Choy, K. (2003). Chemical vapour deposition of coatings. *Progress in materials science, 48*(2), 57-170.

Chung, C.-Y., & Lu, C.-H. (2010). Reverse-microemulsion preparation of visible-light-driven nano-sized $BiVO_4$. *Journal of alloys and compounds, 502*(1), L1-L5.

Chung, D. Y., Jun, S. W., Yoon, G., Kim, H., Yoo, J. M., Lee, K.-S., . . . Kwon, S. G. (2017). Large-scale synthesis of carbon-shell-coated FeP nanoparticles for robust hydrogen evolution reaction electrocatalyst. *Journal of the American Chemical Society, 139*(19), 6669-6674.

Concepcion, P., Reddy, B. M., & Knözinger, H. (1999). FTIR study of low-temperature CO adsorption on pure Al 2 O 3–TiO 2 and V/Al 2 O 3–TiO 2 catalysts. *Physical Chemistry Chemical Physics, 1*(12), 3031-3037.

de Souza, M., Tristao, D., & Corio, P. (2014). Vibrational study of adsorption of Congo red onto TiO 2 and the LSPR effect on its photocatalytic degradation process. *RSC Advances, 4*(44), 23351-23358.

Ding, N., Liu, S., Feng, X., Gao, H., Fang, X., Xu, J., . . . Chen, C. (2009). Hydrothermal growth and characterization of nanostructured vanadium-based oxides. *Crystal Growth and Design, 9*(4), 1723-1728.

Dixit, A., Chen, P., Lawes, G., & Musfeldt, J. (2011). Electronic structure and polaronic excitation in FeVO4. *Applied Physics Letters, 99*(14), 141908.

Dunkle, S. S., Helmich, R. J., & Suslick, K. S. (2009). BiVO4 as a visible-light photocatalyst prepared by ultrasonic spray pyrolysis. *The Journal of Physical Chemistry C, 113*(28), 11980-11983.

Dutta, D. P., Ramakrishnan, M., Roy, M., & Kumar, A. (2017). Effect of transition metal doping on the photocatalytic properties of FeVO4 nanoparticles. *Journal of Photochemistry and Photobiology A: Chemistry, 335*, 102-111.

Fatima, S., Ali, S. I., Iqbal, M. Z., & Rizwan, S. (2017). The high photocatalytic activity and reduced band gap energy of La and Mn co-doped BiFeO 3/graphene nanoplatelet (GNP) nanohybrids. *RSC Advances, 7*(57), 35928-35937.

Ferreira, A., Cemlyn-Jones, J., & Cordeiro, C. R. (2013). Nanoparticles, nanotechnology and pulmonary nanotoxicology. *Revista Portuguesa de Pneumologia (English Edition), 19*(1), 28-37.

Fujihara, K., Izumi, S., Ohno, T., & Matsumura, M. (2000). Time-resolved photoluminescence of particulate TiO2 photocatalysts suspended in aqueous solutions. *Journal of Photochemistry and Photobiology A: Chemistry, 132*(1-2), 99-104.

Fujishima, A., & Honda, K. (1972). Electrochemical photolysis of water at a semiconductor electrode. *Nature, 238*(5358), 37.

Gao, F., Lu, Q., Meng, X., & Komarneni, S. (2008). Synthesis of nanorods and nanowires using biomolecules under conventional-and microwave-hydrothermal conditions. *Journal of materials science, 43*(7), 2377-2386.

Gao, S., Gu, B., Jiao, X., Sun, Y., Zu, X., Yang, F., . . . Ye, B. (2017). Highly efficient and exceptionally durable CO2 photoreduction to methanol over freestanding defective single-unit-cell bismuth vanadate layers. *Journal of the American Chemical Society, 139*(9), 3438-3445.

Ge, L. (2008a). Novel visible-light-driven Pt/BiVO4 photocatalyst for efficient degradation of methyl orange. *Journal of Molecular Catalysis A: Chemical, 282*(1-2), 62-66.

Ge, L. (2008b). Synthesis and characterization of novel visible-light-driven Pd/BiVO4 composite photocatalysts. *Materials Letters, 62*(6-7), 926-928.

Ghiyasiyan-Arani, M., Salavati-Niasari, M., Masjedi-Arani, M., & Mazloom, F. (2018). An easy sonochemical route for synthesis, characterization and photocatalytic performance of nanosized FeVO4 in the presence of aminoacids as green capping agents. *Journal of Materials Science: Materials in Electronics, 29*(1), 474-485.

Ghosh Chaudhuri, R., & Paria, S. (2011). Core/shell nanoparticles: classes, properties, synthesis mechanisms, characterization, and applications. *Chemical Reviews, 112*(4), 2373-2433.

Gotić, M., Musić, S., Ivanda, M., Šoufek, M., & Popović, S. (2005). Synthesis and characterisation of bismuth (III) vanadate. *Journal of Molecular Structure, 744*, 535-540.

Goyal, K., Brar, L. K. G., & Tejoprakash, N. (2010). *Characterization of Selenium Nanostructures Synthesized by Aerobic Microbial Route.*

Gu, S., Li, W., Wang, F., Wang, S., Zhou, H., & Li, H. (2015). Synthesis of buckhorn-like BiVO4 with a shell of CeOx nanodots: Effect of heterojunction structure on the enhancement of photocatalytic activity. *Applied Catalysis B: Environmental, 170*, 186-194.

Guo, H., Guo, D., Zheng, Z., Wen, W., & Chen, J. (2014). Hydrothermal synthesis and visible light photocatalytic activities of Zn 3 (VO 4) 2 nanorods. *Journal of Materials Research, 29*(24), 2934-2941.

Guo, Y., Yang, X., Ma, F., Li, K., Xu, L., Yuan, X., & Guo, Y. (2010). Additive-free controllable fabrication of bismuth vanadates and their photocatalytic activity toward dye degradation. *Applied Surface Science, 256*(7), 2215-2222.

Hadjiivanov, K., Concepción, P., & Knözinger, H. (2000). Analysis of oxidation states of vanadium in vanadia–titania catalysts by the IR spectra of adsorbed NO. *Topics in Catalysis, 11*(1-4), 123-130.

Hanrath, T., & Korgel, B. A. (2002). Nucleation and growth of germanium nanowires seeded by organic monolayer-coated gold nanocrystals. *Journal of the American Chemical Society, 124*(7), 1424-1429.

Hazra, P., Jana, A., Hazra, M., & Datta, J. (2014). Studies on the photo-electrochemical behaviour of Bi 2 S 3 NPs embedded in a PANINFs matrix. *RSC Advances, 4*(64), 33662-33671.

Hoar, T., & Schulman, J. (1943). Transparent water-in-oil dispersions: the oleopathic hydro-micelle. *Nature, 152*(3847), 102.

Hoard, J., Scheidt, W. R., & Tsai, C.-C. (1971). Stereochemistry of dioxovanadium (V) complexes. I. Crystal and molecular structure of triammonium bis (oxalato) dioxovanadate (V) dihydrate. *Journal of the American Chemical Society, 93*(16), 3867-3872.

Hofmann, M., Rainer, M., Schulze, S., Hietschold, M., & Mehring, M. (2015). Nonaqueous Synthesis of a Bismuth Vanadate Photocatalyst By Using Microwave Heating: Photooxidation versus Photosensitized Decomposition in Visible-Light-Driven Photocatalysis. *ChemCatChem, 7*(8), 1357-1365.

Hu, C., Xu, J., Zhu, Y., Chen, A., Bian, Z., & Wang, H. (2016). Morphological effect of BiVO4 catalysts on degradation of aqueous paracetamol under visible light irradiation. *Environmental Science and Pollution Research, 23*(18), 18421-18428.

Hu, J., Yu, Y., Guo, H., Chen, Z., Li, A., Feng, X., . . . Hu, G. (2011). Sol–gel hydrothermal synthesis and enhanced biosensing properties of nanoplated lanthanum-substituted bismuth titanate microspheres. *Journal of Materials Chemistry, 21*(14), 5352-5359.

Hu, S. J., Yang, J., & Liao, X. H. (2013). *Highly efficient degradation of methylene blue on microwave synthesized FeVO4 nanoparticles photocatalysts under visible-light irradiation.* Paper presented at the Applied Mechanics and Materials.

Hu, Y., Chen, W., Fu, J., Ba, M., Sun, F., Zhang, P., & Zou, J. (2018). Hydrothermal synthesis of BiVO4/TiO2 composites and their application for degradation of gaseous benzene under visible light irradiation. *Applied Surface Science, 436*, 319-326.

Huang, S.-T., Jiang, Y.-R., Chou, S.-Y., Dai, Y.-M., & Chen, C.-C. (2014). Synthesis, characterization, photocatalytic activity of visible-light-responsive photocatalysts BiOxCly/BiOmBrn by controlled hydrothermal method. *Journal of Molecular Catalysis A: Chemical, 391*, 105-120.

Hubert, M., Martin, S., Yacobi, B. G., Burgmann, T. A., & Passy, P. W. (2011). Phototherapeutic treatment method using a passive host medium containing nanoparticles: Google Patents.

Imam, S. S., Zango, Z. U., & Abdullahi, H. (2018). Room Temperature Synthesis of Bismuth Oxyiodide with Different Morphologies for the Photocatalytic Degradation of Norfloxacin. *American Scientific Research Journal for Engineering, Technology, and Sciences (ASRJETS), 41*(1), 26-39.

Irfan, S., Li, L., Saleemi, A. S., & Nan, C.-W. (2017). Enhanced photocatalytic activity of La 3+ and Se 4+ co-doped bismuth ferrite nanostructures. *Journal of Materials Chemistry A, 5*(22), 11143-11151.

Irfan, S., Shen, Y., Rizwan, S., Wang, H. C., Khan, S. B., & Nan, C. W. (2017). Band-Gap Engineering and Enhanced Photocatalytic Activity of Sm and Mn Doped BiFeO3 Nanoparticles. *Journal of the American Ceramic Society, 100*(1), 31-40.

Jiang, Y.-R., Chou, S.-Y., Chang, J.-L., Huang, S.-T., Lin, H.-P., & Chen, C.-C. (2015). Hydrothermal synthesis of bismuth oxybromide–bismuth oxyiodide composites with high visible light photocatalytic performance for the degradation of CV and phenol. *RSC Advances, 5*(39), 30851-30860.

Jo, W. J., Kang, H. J., Kong, K.-J., Lee, Y. S., Park, H., Lee, Y., . . . Lee, J. S. (2015). Phase transition-induced band edge engineering of BiVO4 to split pure water under visible light. *Proceedings of the National Academy of Sciences, 112*(45), 13774-13778.

Joung, S.-K., Amemiya, T., Murabayashi, M., & Itoh, K. (2006). Relation between photocatalytic activity and preparation conditions for nitrogen-doped visible light-driven TiO2 photocatalysts. *Applied Catalysis A: General, 312*, 20-26.

Ju-Nam, Y., & Lead, J. R. (2008). Manufactured nanoparticles: an overview of their chemistry, interactions and potential environmental implications. *Science of the total environment, 400*(1-3), 396-414.

Kango, S., Kalia, S., Celli, A., Njuguna, J., Habibi, Y., & Kumar, R. (2013). Surface modification of inorganic nanoparticles for development of organic–inorganic nanocomposites—a review. *Progress in Polymer Science, 38*(8), 1232-1261.

Kar, A., Kundu, S., & Patra, A. (2012). Photocatalytic properties of semiconductor SnO 2/CdS heterostructure nanocrystals. *RSC Advances, 2*(27), 10222-10230.

Kar, A., Sain, S., Kundu, S., Bhattacharyya, A., Kumar Pradhan, S., & Patra, A. (2015). Influence of size and shape on the photocatalytic properties of SnO2 nanocrystals. *ChemPhysChem, 16*(5), 1017-1025.

Ke, D., Peng, T., Ma, L., Cai, P., & Dai, K. (2009). Effects of hydrothermal temperature on the microstructures of BiVO4 and its photocatalytic O2 evolution activity under visible light. *Inorganic Chemistry, 48*(11), 4685-4691.

Ke, D., Peng, T., Ma, L., Cai, P., & Jiang, P. (2008). Photocatalytic water splitting for O2 production under visible-light irradiation on BiVO4 nanoparticles in different sacrificial reagent solutions. *Applied Catalysis A: General, 350*(1), 111-117.

Khan, S. A., Khan, S. B., & Asiri, A. M. (2016). Layered double hydroxide of Cd-Al/C for the Mineralization and De-coloration of Dyes in Solar and Visible Light Exposure. *Scientific Reports, 6*, 35107.

Khan, S. B., Hou, M., Shuang, S., & Zhang, Z. (2017). Morphological influence of TiO2 nanostructures (nanozigzag, nanohelics and nanorod) on photocatalytic degradation of organic dyes. *Applied Surface Science, 400*, 184-193.

Kim, H. Y., Park, J., & Yang, H. (2003). Synthesis of silicon nitride nanowires directly from the silicon substrates. *Chemical Physics Letters, 372*(1-2), 269-274.

Kohtani, S., Tomohiro, M., Tokumura, K., & Nakagaki, R. (2005). Photooxidation reactions of polycyclic aromatic hydrocarbons over pure and Ag-loaded BiVO4 photocatalysts. *Applied Catalysis B: Environmental, 58*(3-4), 265-272.

Kortüm, G., Braun, W., & Herzog, G. (1963). Principles and Techniques of Diffuse-Reflectance Spectroscopy. *Angewandte Chemie International Edition in English, 2*(7), 333-341.

Krahne, R., Morello, G., Figuerola, A., George, C., Deka, S., & Manna, L. (2011). Physical properties of elongated inorganic nanoparticles. *Physics Reports, 501*(3-5), 75-221.

Krystek, P., Ulrich, A., Garcia, C. C., Manohar, S., & Ritsema, R. (2011). Application of plasma spectrometry for the analysis of engineered nanoparticles in suspensions and products. *Journal of analytical atomic spectrometry, 26*(9), 1701-1721.

Kubelka, P., & Munk, F. (1931). An article on optics of paint layers. *Z. Tech. Phys, 12*(593-601).

Kudo, A., Omori, K., & Kato, H. (1999). A novel aqueous process for preparation of crystal form-controlled and highly crystalline BiVO4 powder from layered vanadates at room temperature and its photocatalytic and photophysical properties. *Journal of the American Chemical Society, 121*(49), 11459-11467.

Lam, S.-M., Sin, J.-C., & Mohamed, A. R. (2016). A review on photocatalytic application of g-C3N4/semiconductor (CNS) nanocomposites towards the erasure of dyeing wastewater. *Materials Science in Semiconductor Processing, 47*, 62-84.

Lamm, B., Sarkar, A., & Stefik, M. (2017). Surface functionalized atomic layer deposition of bismuth vanadate for single-phase scheelite. *Journal of Materials Chemistry A, 5*(13), 6060-6069.

Lee, A.-H., Wang, Y.-C., & Chen, C.-C. (2019). Composite photocatalyst, tetragonal lead bismuth oxyiodide/bismuth oxyiodide/graphitic carbon nitride: Synthesis, characterization, and photocatalytic activity. *Journal of colloid and interface science, 533*, 319-332.

Lee, D. K., Cho, I.-S., Lee, S., Bae, S.-T., Noh, J. H., Kim, D. W., & Hong, K. S. (2010). Effects of carbon content on the photocatalytic activity of C/BiVO4 composites under visible light irradiation. *Materials Chemistry and Physics, 119*(1-2), 106-111.

Lee, W. W., Lu, C.-S., Chuang, C.-W., Chen, Y.-J., Fu, J.-Y., Siao, C.-W., & Chen, C.-C. (2015). Synthesis of bismuth oxyiodides and their composites: characterization, photocatalytic activity, and degradation mechanisms. *RSC Advances, 5*(30), 23450-23463.

Lee, Y.-H., Dai, Y.-M., Fu, J.-Y., & Chen, C.-C. (2017). A series of bismuth-oxychloride/bismuth-oxyiodide/graphene-oxide nanocomposites: Synthesis, characterization, and photcatalytic activity and mechanism. *Molecular Catalysis, 432*, 196-209.

Lehnen, T., Valldor, M., Nižňanský, D., & Mathur, S. (2014). Hydrothermally grown porous FeVO 4 nanorods and their integration as active material in gas-sensing devices. *Journal of Materials Chemistry A, 2*(6), 1862-1868.

Li, G., Zhang, D., & Yu, J. C. (2008). Ordered mesoporous BiVO4 through nanocasting: a superior visible light-driven photocatalyst. *Chemistry of Materials, 20*(12), 3983-3992.

Li, H., Liu, G., & Duan, X. (2009). Monoclinic BiVO4 with regular morphologies: hydrothermal synthesis, characterization and photocatalytic properties. *Materials Chemistry and Physics, 115*(1), 9-13.

Li, J.-Q., Guo, Z.-Y., Wang, D.-F., Lui, H., Du, J., & Zhu, Z.-F. (2014). Effects of pH value on the surface morphology of BiVO4 microspheres and removal of methylene blue under visible light. *Journal of Experimental Nanoscience, 9*(6), 616-624.

Li, J., Cui, M., Guo, Z., Liu, Z., & Zhu, Z. (2014). Synthesis of dumbbell-like CuO–BiVO4 heterogeneous nanostructures with enhanced visible-light photocatalytic activity. *Materials Letters, 130*, 36-39.

Li, W., Wang, X., Wang, Z., Meng, Y., Sun, X., Yan, T., . . . Kong, D. (2016). Relationship between crystalline phases and photocatalytic activities of BiVO4. *Materials Research Bulletin, 83*, 259-267.

Li, X., Zou, M., & Wang, Y. (2017). Soft-Template Synthesis of Mesoporous Anatase TiO2 Nanospheres and Its Enhanced Photoactivity. *Molecules, 22*(11), 1943.

Li, Y., Zhang, W., Li, L., Yi, C., Lv, H., & Song, Q. (2016). Litchi-like CdS/CdTiO 3–TiO 2 composite: synthesis and enhanced photocatalytic performance for crystal violet degradation and hydrogen production. *RSC Advances, 6*(56), 51374-51386.

Lidström, P., Tierney, J., Wathey, B., & Westman, J. (2001). Microwave assisted organic synthesis—a review. *Tetrahedron, 57*(45), 9225-9283.

Lin, H.-P., Chen, C.-C., Lee, W. W., Lai, Y.-Y., Chen, J.-Y., Chen, Y.-Q., & Fu, J.-Y. (2016). Synthesis of a SrFeO 3− x/gC 3 N 4 heterojunction with improved visible-light photocatalytic activities in chloramphenicol and crystal violet degradation. *RSC Advances, 6*(3), 2323-2336.

Lin, X., Liu, Z., Guo, X., Liu, C., Zhai, H., Wang, Q., & Chang, L. (2014). Controllable synthesis and photocatalytic activity of spherical, flower-like and nanofibrous bismuth tungstates. *Materials Science and Engineering: B, 188*, 35-42.

Linsebigler, A. L., Lu, G., & Yates Jr, J. T. (1995). Photocatalysis on TiO2 surfaces: principles, mechanisms, and selected results. *Chemical Reviews, 95*(3), 735-758.

Liqiang, J., Yichun, Q., Baiqi, W., Shudan, L., Baojiang, J., Libin, Y., . . . Jiazhong, S. (2006). Review of photoluminescence performance of nano-sized semiconductor materials and its relationships with photocatalytic activity. *Solar Energy Materials and Solar Cells, 90*(12), 1773-1787.

Liu, B., Lin, L., Yu, D., Sun, J., Zhu, Z., Gao, P., & Wang, W. (2018). Construction of fiber-based BiVO 4/SiO 2/reduced graphene oxide (RGO) with efficient visible light photocatalytic activity. *Cellulose, 25*(2), 1089-1101.

Liu, C. J., & Xu, Y. H. (2011). *Synthesis, Characterization and Photocatalytic Activities of Bismuth Vanadate by Facile Co-Precipitation Method.* Paper presented at the Advanced Materials Research.

Liu, D., Zi, W., Sajjad, S. D., Hsu, C., Shen, Y., Wei, M., & Liu, F. (2015). Reversible electron storage in an all-vanadium photoelectrochemical storage cell: synergy between vanadium redox and hybrid photocatalyst. *Acs Catalysis, 5*(4), 2632-2639.

Liu, F.-Y., Jiang, Y.-R., Chen, C.-C., & Lee, W. W. (2018). Novel synthesis of PbBiO2Cl/BiOCl nanocomposite with enhanced visible-driven-light photocatalytic activity. *Catalysis today, 300*, 112-123.

Liu, F.-Y., Lin, J.-H., Dai, Y.-M., Chen, L.-W., Huang, S.-T., Yeh, T.-W., . . . Chen, C.-C. (2018a). Preparation of perovskites PbBiO2I/PbO exhibiting visible-light photocatalytic activity. *Catalysis today*.

Liu, F.-Y., Lin, J.-H., Dai, Y.-M., Chen, L.-W., Huang, S.-T., Yeh, T.-W., . . . Chen, C.-C. (2018b). Preparation of perovskites PbBiO2I/PbO exhibiting visible-light photocatalytic activity. *Catalysis today, 314*, 28-41.

Liu, H., Cheng, X., Liu, H., Yang, J., Cao, J., Liu, Y., . . . Fei, L. (2013). Influence of annealing temperature on structural, optical and magnetic properties of ZnO. 97Cu0. 01V0. 02O nanoparticles. *Journal of Materials Science: Materials in Electronics, 24*(1), 317-323.

Liu, H., Nakamura, R., & Nakato, Y. (2005). Promoted photo-oxidation reactivity of particulate BiVO4 photocatalyst prepared by a photoassisted sol-gel method. *Journal of the Electrochemical Society, 152*(11), G856-G861.

Liu, J., Cheng, B., & Yu, J. (2016). A new understanding of the photocatalytic mechanism of the direct Z-scheme gC 3 N 4/TiO 2 heterostructure. *Physical Chemistry Chemical Physics, 18*(45), 31175-31183.

Liu, M., Xue, X., Yu, S., Wang, X., Hu, X., Tian, H., . . . Zheng, W. (2017). Improving Photocatalytic Performance from Bi 2 WO 6@ MoS 2/graphene Hybrids via Gradual Charge Transferred Pathway. *Scientific Reports, 7*(1), 3637.

Liu, M., Yu, Y. X., & Zhang, W. D. (2017). A Non-enzymatic Hydrogen Peroxide Photoelectrochemical Sensor Based on a BiVO4 Electrode. *Electroanalysis, 29*(1), 305-311.

Liu, W., Cao, L., Su, G., Liu, H., Wang, X., & Zhang, L. (2010). Ultrasound assisted synthesis of monoclinic structured spindle BiVO4 particles with hollow structure and its photocatalytic property. *Ultrasonics sonochemistry, 17*(4), 669-674.

Llordes, A., Hammack, A. T., Buonsanti, R., Tangirala, R., Aloni, S., Helms, B. A., & Milliron, D. J. (2011). Polyoxometalates and colloidal nanocrystals as building blocks for metal oxide nanocomposite films. *Journal of Materials Chemistry, 21*(31), 11631-11638.

Luo, L., Fei, Y., Chen, K., Li, D., Wang, X., Wang, Q., . . . Qiao, H. (2015). Facile synthesis of one-dimensional zinc vanadate nanofibers for high lithium storage anode material. *Journal of alloys and compounds, 649*, 1019-1024.

Ma, D.-K., Guan, M.-L., Liu, S.-S., Zhang, Y.-Q., Zhang, C.-W., He, Y.-X., & Huang, S.-M. (2012). Controlled synthesis of olive-shaped Bi$_2$S$_3$/BiVO$_4$ microspheres through a limited chemical conversion route and enhanced visible-light-responding photocatalytic activity. *Dalton Transactions, 41*(18), 5581-5586.

Ma, D., Wang, S., Cai, P., Jiang, J., Yang, D., & Huang, S. (2009). Self-assembled three-dimensional hierarchical BiVO4 microspheres from nanoplates: malic acid-assisted hydrothermal synthesis and photocatalytic activities. *Chemistry letters, 38*(10), 962-963.

Madhusudan, P., Yu, J., Wang, W., Cheng, B., & Liu, G. (2012). Facile synthesis of novel hierarchical graphene–Bi$_2$O$_2$CO$_3$ composites with enhanced photocatalytic performance under visible light. *Dalton Transactions, 41*(47), 14345-14353.

Malwal, D., & Gopinath, P. (2016). Enhanced photocatalytic activity of hierarchical three dimensional metal oxide@ CuO nanostructures towards the degradation of Congo red dye under solar radiation. *Catalysis Science & Technology, 6*(12), 4458-4472.

Mandal, H., Shyamal, S., Hajra, P., Bera, A., Sariket, D., Kundu, S., & Bhattacharya, C. (2016). Development of ternary iron vanadium oxide semiconductors for applications in photoelectrochemical water oxidation. *RSC Advances, 6*(6), 4992-4999.

Mao, L.-j., Liu, C.-y., & Li, J. (2008). Template-free synthesis of VO x hierarchical hollow spheres. *Journal of Materials Chemistry, 18*(14), 1640-1643.

Martinez-de La Cruz, A., & Perez, U. G. (2010). Photocatalytic properties of BiVO4 prepared by the co-precipitation method: Degradation of rhodamine B and possible reaction mechanisms under visible irradiation. *Materials Research Bulletin, 45*(2), 135-141.

Melghit, K., Belloui, B., & Yahya, A. H. (1999). Room temperature synthesis of zinc pyrovanadate Zn$_3$(OH)$_2$V$_2$O$_7\cdot$2H$_2$O. *Journal of Materials Chemistry, 9*(7), 1543-1545.

Meng, Q., Lv, H., Yuan, M., Chen, Z., Chen, Z., & Wang, X. (2017). In Situ Hydrothermal Construction of Direct Solid-State Nano-Z-Scheme BiVO4/Pyridine-Doped g-C3N4 Photocatalyst with Efficient Visible-Light-Induced Photocatalytic Degradation of Phenol and Dyes. *ACS Omega, 2*(6), 2728-2739.

Merupo, V., Velumani, S., Oza, G., Makowska-Janusik, M., & Kassiba, A. (2015). Structural, electronic and optical features of molybdenum-doped bismuth vanadium oxide. *Materials Science in Semiconductor Processing, 31*, 618-623.

Merupo, V. I., Velumani, S., Oza, G., Tabellout, M., Bizarro, M., Coste, S., & Kassiba, A. H. (2016). High Energy Ball-Milling Synthesis of Nanostructured Ag-Doped and BiVO4-Based Photocatalysts. *ChemistrySelect, 1*(6), 1278-1286.

Mikhailik, V., & Kraus, H. (2006). Cryogenic scintillators in searches for extremely rare events. *Journal of Physics D: Applied Physics, 39*(6), 1181.

Mittal, A. K., Chisti, Y., & Banerjee, U. C. (2013). Synthesis of metallic nanoparticles using plant extracts. *Biotechnology advances, 31*(2), 346-356.

Mohamed, H. H., & Bahnemann, D. W. (2012). The role of electron transfer in photocatalysis: Fact and fictions. *Applied Catalysis B: Environmental, 128*, 91-104.

Mohamed, R., McKinney, D., & Sigmund, W. (2012). Enhanced nanocatalysts. *Materials Science and Engineering: R: Reports, 73*(1), 1-13.

Morose, G. (2010). The 5 principles of "design for safer nanotechnology". *Journal of Cleaner Production, 18*(3), 285-289.

Moscow, S., & Jothivenkatachalam, K. (2016). Facile microwave assisted synthesis of floral-shaped BiVO 4 nano particles for their photocatalytic and photoelectrochemical performances. *Journal of Materials Science: Materials in Electronics, 27*(2), 1433-1443.

Moscow, S., Jothivenkatachalam, K., & Jaganathan, K. (2012). Facile fabrication, Characterization of Bismuth vanadate nanoparticles via hydrothermal method and its photocatalytic properties. *STRUCTURAL AND OPTICAL STUDY OF TITANIUM DIOXIDE THIN FILMS PREPARED BY SOL–GEL TECHNIQUE, 24*(3), 46.

Nagaveni, K., Sivalingam, G., Hegde, M., & Madras, G. (2004). Photocatalytic degradation of organic compounds over combustion-synthesized nano-TiO2. *Environmental science & technology, 38*(5), 1600-1604.

Narayan, H., Alemu, H., Alotsi, D. N., Macheli, L., Thakurdesai, M., Jaybhaye, S., & Singh, A. (2011). Fast and complete degradation of Congo red under visible light with Er3+ and Nd3+ ions doped TiO2 nanocomposites. *Nanotechnology Development, 2*(1), 2.

Nguyen, D. T., & Hong, S.-S. (2017). The Effect of Solvent on the Synthesis of BiVO4 Using Solvothermal Method and Their Photocatalytic Activity Under Visible Light Irradiation. *Topics in Catalysis, 60*(9-11), 782-788.

Ni, S., Wang, X., Zhou, G., Yang, F., Wang, J., & He, D. (2010). Crystallized Zn3 (VO4) 2: synthesis, characterization and optical property. *Journal of alloys and compounds, 491*(1-2), 378-381.

Nikam, S., & Joshi, S. (2016). Irreversible phase transition in BiVO 4 nanostructures synthesized by a polyol method and enhancement in photo degradation of methylene blue. *RSC Advances, 6*(109), 107463-107474.

Nithya, V., & Selvan, R. K. (2011). Synthesis, electrical and dielectric properties of FeVO4 nanoparticles. *Physica B: Condensed Matter, 406*(1), 24-29.

Niu, J., Ding, S., Zhang, L., Zhao, J., & Feng, C. (2013). Visible-light-mediated Sr-Bi 2 O 3 photocatalysis of tetracycline: kinetics, mechanisms and toxicity assessment. *Chemosphere, 93*(1), 1-8.

Nong, Q., Cui, M., Lin, H., Zhao, L., & He, Y. (2015). Fabrication, characterization and photocatalytic activity of gC 3 N 4 coupled with FeVO 4 nanorods. *RSC Advances, 5*(35), 27933-27939.

Pei, L., Lin, N., Wei, T., Liu, H., & Yu, H. (2015). Formation of copper vanadate nanobelts and their electrochemical behaviors for the determination of ascorbic acid. *Journal of Materials Chemistry A, 3*(6), 2690-2700.

Pei, L., Lin, N., Wei, T., Liu, H., & Yu, H. (2015). Zinc vanadate nanorods and their visible light photocatalytic activity. *Journal of alloys and compounds, 631*, 90-98.

Pei, L., Wang, S., Jiang, Y., Xie, Y., Li, Y., & Guo, Y. (2013). Single crystalline Sr germanate nanowires and their photocatalytic performance for the degradation of methyl blue. *CrystEngComm, 15*(38), 7815-7823.

Peng, Y., Hou, L., & Yuan, C. (2008). Preparation and Photocatalytic Property of BiVO~4 Micro-rods with Brick Shape. *Chinese Journal of Applied Chemistry, 25*(4), 485.

Pingmuang, K., Nattestad, A., Chen, J., Kangwansupamonkon, W., & Phanichphant, S. (2016). Photocatalytic Degradation of Methylene Blue by Innovative BiVO4/TiO2 Composite Films under Visible Light Irradiation. *J. Environ. Sci., 3*, 1-8.

Pitale, S. S., Gohain, M., Nagpure, I., Ntwaeaborwa, O., Bezuidenhoudt, B. C., & Swart, H. (2012). A comparative study on structural, morphological and luminescence characteristics of Zn3 (VO4) 2 phosphor prepared via hydrothermal and citrate-gel combustion routes. *Physica B: Condensed Matter, 407*(10), 1485-1488.

Pookmanee, P., Kojinok, S., & Phanichphant, S. (2014). Photocatalytic Degradation of 2, 4-dichlorophenol using BiVO4 Powder Prepared by the Sol–gel Method. *Transactions of the Materials Research Society of Japan, 39*(4), 431-434.

Prasad, K. S., Patel, H., Patel, T., Patel, K., & Selvaraj, K. (2013). Biosynthesis of Se nanoparticles and its effect on UV-induced DNA damage. *Colloids and Surfaces B: Biointerfaces, 103*, 261-266.

Qu, X., Alvarez, P. J., & Li, Q. (2013). Applications of nanotechnology in water and wastewater treatment. *Water research, 47*(12), 3931-3946.

Radad, K., Al-Shraim, M., Moldzio, R., & Rausch, W.-D. (2012). Recent advances in benefits and hazards of engineered nanoparticles. *Environmental toxicology and pharmacology, 34*(3), 661-672.

Rao, H., Lu, Z., Liu, X., Ge, H., Zhang, Z., Zou, P., . . . Wang, Y. (2016). Visible light-driven photocatalytic degradation performance for methylene blue with different multi-morphological features of ZnS. *RSC Advances, 6*(52), 46299-46307.

Rejniak, L., & Piotrowska, H. (1966). Effect of malachite green, congo red and safranin on cell division in gemmae of allium cepa. *Nature, 209*(5022), 517.

Ren, L., Jin, L., Wang, J.-B., Yang, F., Qiu, M.-Q., & Yu, Y. (2009). Template-free synthesis of BiVO4 nanostructures: I. Nanotubes with hexagonal cross sections by oriented attachment and their photocatalytic property for water splitting under visible light. *Nanotechnology, 20*(11), 115603.

Roco, M. C. (2017). Overview: Affirmation of Nanotechnology between 2000 and 2030. *Nanotechnology Commercialization: Manufacturing Processes and Products*, 1-23.

Sajid, M. M., Khan, S. B., Shad, N. A., Amin, N., & Zhang, Z. (2018). Visible light assisted photocatalytic degradation of crystal violet dye and electrochemical detection of ascorbic acid using a BiVO 4/FeVO 4 heterojunction composite. *RSC Advances, 8*(42), 23489-23498.

Samuelson, L. (2003). Self-forming nanoscale devices. *Materials today, 6*(10), 22-31.

Sánchez, A., Recillas, S., Font, X., Casals, E., González, E., & Puntes, V. (2011). Ecotoxicity of, and remediation with, engineered inorganic nanoparticles in the environment. *TrAC Trends in Analytical Chemistry, 30*(3), 507-516.

Sathyanarayana, D., & Patel, C. (1964). Studies of ammonium dioxovanadium (V) bisoxalate dihydrate. *Bulletin of the Chemical Society of Japan, 37*(12), 1736-1740.

Sayama, K., Nomura, A., Arai, T., Sugita, T., Abe, R., Yanagida, M., . . . Sugihara, H. (2006). Photoelectrochemical decomposition of water into H2 and O2 on porous BiVO4 thin-film electrodes under visible light and significant effect of Ag ion treatment. *The Journal of Physical Chemistry B, 110*(23), 11352-11360.

Schoiswohl, J., Surnev, S., Netzer, F., & Kresse, G. (2006). Vanadium oxide nanostructures: from zero-to three-dimensional. *Journal of Physics: Condensed Matter, 18*(4), R1.

Seliverstov, A., & Streb, C. (2014). A New Class of Homogeneous Visible-Light Photocatalysts: Molecular Cerium Vanadium Oxide Clusters. *Chemistry–A European Journal, 20*(31), 9733-9738.

Shang, M., Wang, W., Sun, S., Ren, J., Zhou, L., & Zhang, L. (2009). Efficient visible light-induced photocatalytic degradation of contaminant by spindle-like PANI/BiVO4. *The Journal of Physical Chemistry C, 113*(47), 20228-20233.

Shang, M., Wang, W., Zhou, L., Sun, S., & Yin, W. (2009). Nanosized BiVO4 with high visible-light-induced photocatalytic activity: ultrasonic-assisted synthesis and protective effect of surfactant. *Journal of hazardous materials, 172*(1), 338-344.

Shchukin, V., Ledentsov, N. N., & Bimberg, D. (2013). *Epitaxy of nanostructures*: Springer Science & Business Media.

Shi, W., Yan, Y., & Yan, X. (2013). Microwave-assisted synthesis of nano-scale BiVO4 photocatalysts and their excellent visible-light-driven photocatalytic activity for the degradation of ciprofloxacin. *Chemical engineering journal, 215*, 740-746.

Shifu, C., Wei, Z., Wei, L., & Sujuan, Z. (2009). Preparation, characterization and activity evaluation of p–n junction photocatalyst p-NiO/n-ZnO. *Journal of sol-gel science and technology, 50*(3), 387-396.

Shinde, D. R., Tambade, P. S., Chaskar, M. G., & Gadave, K. M. (2017). Photocatalytic degradation of dyes in water by analytical reagent grades ZnO, TiO 2 and SnO 2: a comparative study. *Drinking Water Engineering and Science, 10*(2), 109.

Siao, C.-W., Chen, H.-L., Chen, L.-W., Chang, J.-L., Yeh, T.-W., & Chen, C.-C. (2018). Controlled Hydrothermal Synthesis of Bismuth Oxychloride/Bismuth Oxybromide/Bismuth Oxyiodide Composites Exhibiting Visible-Light Photocatalytic Degradation of 2-Hydroxybenzoic Acid and Crystal Violet. *Journal of colloid and interface science.*

Sivakumar, J., Premkumar, C., Santhanam, P., & Saraswathi, N. (2011). Biosynthesis of silver nanoparticles using Calotropis gigantean leaf. *African Journal of Basic & Applied Sciences, 3*(6), 265-270.

Sivakumar, V., Suresh, R., Giribabu, K., & Narayanan, V. (2015). BiVO4 nanoparticles: Preparation, characterization and photocatalytic activity. *Cogent Chemistry, 1*(1), 1074647.

Strobel, R., Metz, H. J., & Pratsinis, S. E. (2008). Brilliant yellow, transparent pure, and SiO2-coated BiVO4 nanoparticles made in flames. *Chemistry of Materials, 20*(20), 6346-6351.

Su, J., Liu, C., Liu, D., Li, M., & Zhou, J. (2016). Enhanced Photoelectrochemical Performance of the BiVO4/Zn: BiVO4 Homojunction for Water Oxidation. *ChemCatChem, 8*(20), 3279-3286.

Sun, J., Chen, G., Wu, J., Dong, H., & Xiong, G. (2013). Bismuth vanadate hollow spheres: Bubble template synthesis and enhanced photocatalytic properties for photodegradation. *Applied Catalysis B: Environmental, 132*, 304-314.

Sun, S., Wang, W., Zhou, L., & Xu, H. (2009). Efficient methylene blue removal over hydrothermally synthesized starlike BiVO4. *Industrial & Engineering Chemistry Research, 48*(4), 1735-1739.

Tang, J., Cheng, G., Zhou, H., Yang, H., Lu, Z., & Chen, R. (2012). Shape-dependent photocatalytic activities of bismuth subcarbonate nanostructures. *Journal of nanoscience and nanotechnology, 12*(5), 4028-4034.

Thakkar, K. N., Mhatre, S. S., & Parikh, R. Y. (2010). Biological synthesis of metallic nanoparticles. *Nanomedicine: Nanotechnology, Biology and Medicine, 6*(2), 257-262.

Thalluri, S., Martinez-Suarez, C., Virga, A., Russo, N., & Saracco, G. (2013). Insights from crystal size and band gap on the catalytic activity of monoclinic BiVO4. *International Journal of Chemical Engineering and Applications, 4*(5), 305.

Thomas, J. M. (1994). Turning points in catalysis. *Angewandte Chemie International Edition in English, 33*(9), 913-937.

Tracey, A. S., Gresser, M. J., & Parkinson, K. M. (1987). Vanadium (V) oxyanions. Interactions of vanadate with oxalate, lactate and glycerate. *Inorganic Chemistry, 26*(5), 629-638.

Trommer, R. M., & Bergmann, C. P. (2015). History of Flame Spray (FS) Technique *Flame Spray Technology* (pp. 7-10): Springer.

Ullah, H., Tahir, A. A., & Mallick, T. K. (2018). Structural and electronic properties of oxygen defective and Se-doped p-type BiVO4 (001) thin film for the applications of photocatalysis. *Applied Catalysis B: Environmental, 224*, 895-903.

Venkatesan, R., Velumani, S., Ordon, K., Makowska-Janusik, M., Corbel, G., & Kassiba, A. (2018). Nanostructured bismuth vanadate (BiVO 4) thin films for efficient visible light photocatalysis. *Materials Chemistry and Physics, 205*, 325-333.

Vuk, A. Š., Orel, B., & Dražič, G. (2001). IR spectroelectrochemical studies of Fe 2 V 4 O 13, FeVO 4 and InVO 4 thin films obtained via sol-gel synthesis. *Journal of Solid State Electrochemistry, 5*(7-8), 437-449.

Wang, C.-T., Lai, D.-L., & Chen, M.-T. (2010). Synthesis of iron-doped vanadium–tin oxide nanocrystallites for CO gas sensing. *Materials Letters, 64*(1), 65-67.

Wang, F., Shao, M., Cheng, L., Hua, J., & Wei, X. (2009). The synthesis of monoclinic bismuth vanadate nanoribbons and studies of photoconductive, photoresponse, and photocatalytic properties. *Materials Research Bulletin, 44*(8), 1687-1691.

Wang, G., Ling, Y., & Li, Y. (2012). Oxygen-deficient metal oxide nanostructures for photoelectrochemical water oxidation and other applications. *Nanoscale, 4*(21), 6682-6691.

Wang, L. (2017). Electrochemically-Treated BiVO4 Photoanode for Efficient Photoelectrochemical Water Splitting. *Angewandte Chemie.*

Wang, M., Liu, Q., Che, Y., Zhang, L., & Zhang, D. (2013). Characterization and photocatalytic properties of N-doped BiVO4 synthesized via a sol–gel method. *Journal of alloys and compounds, 548*, 70-76.

Wang, M., Shi, Y., & Jiang, G. (2012). 3D hierarchical Zn 3 (OH) 2 V 2 O 7 · 2H 2 O and Zn 3 (VO 4) 2 microspheres: Synthesis, characterization and photoluminescence. *Materials Research Bulletin, 47*(1), 18-23.

Wang, S., Guan, Y., Wang, L., Zhao, W., He, H., Xiao, J., . . . Sun, C. (2015). Fabrication of a novel bifunctional material of BiOI/Ag3VO4 with high adsorption–photocatalysis for efficient treatment of dye wastewater. *Applied Catalysis B: Environmental, 168*, 448-457.

Wang, S., Li, D., Sun, C., Yang, S., Guan, Y., & He, H. (2014). Synthesis and characterization of g-C3N4/Ag3VO4 composites with significantly enhanced visible-light photocatalytic activity for triphenylmethane dye degradation. *Applied Catalysis B: Environmental, 144*, 885-892.

Wang, Z., Feng, Y., Cao, L., Xue, M., Shen, K., & Zheng, M. (2018). Preparation and optical properties of Bi2FeVMoO10 nanoparticles structurally derived from cation-substitutions in Scheelite-type BiVO4. *Materials Research Bulletin, 100*, 145-152.

Weckhuysen, B. M., & Keller, D. E. (2003). Chemistry, spectroscopy and the role of supported vanadium oxides in heterogeneous catalysis. *Catalysis today, 78*(1-4), 25-46.

Weisbuch, C., & Vinter, B. (2014). *Quantum semiconductor structures: fundamentals and applications*: Elsevier.

Whittaker, A., & Mingos, D. (1994). The application of microwave heating to chemical syntheses. *Journal of Microwave Power and Electromagnetic Energy, 29*(4), 195-219.

Wong, C. L., Tan, Y. N., & Mohamed, A. R. (2011). A review on the formation of titania nanotube photocatalysts by hydrothermal treatment. *Journal of environmental management, 92*(7), 1669-1680.

Wu, T., Lin, T., Zhao, J., Hidaka, H., & Serpone, N. (1999). TiO2-assisted photodegradation of dyes. 9. Photooxidation of a squarylium cyanine dye in aqueous dispersions under visible light irradiation. *Environmental science & technology, 33*(9), 1379-1387.

Wu, Y.-C., Chaing, Y.-C., Huang, C.-Y., Wang, S.-F., & Yang, H.-Y. (2013). Morphology-controllable Bi2O3 crystals through an aqueous precipitation method and their photocatalytic performance. *Dyes and Pigments, 98*(1), 25-30.

Xi, G., & Ye, J. (2010). Synthesis of bismuth vanadate nanoplates with exposed {001} facets and enhanced visible-light photocatalytic properties. *Chemical Communications, 46*(11), 1893-1895.

Xiao, B.-C., Lin, L.-Y., Hong, J.-Y., Lin, H.-S., & Song, Y.-T. (2017). Synthesis of a monoclinic BiVO 4 nanorod array as the photocatalyst for efficient photoelectrochemical water oxidation. *RSC Advances, 7*(13), 7547-7554.

Xie, B., He, C., Cai, P., & Xiong, Y. (2010). Preparation of monoclinic BiVO4 thin film by citrate route for photocatalytic application under visible light. *Thin Solid Films, 518*(8), 1958-1961.

Xu, C., Zhu, G., Wu, J., & Liang, J. (2014). Template-free hydrothermal synthesis different morphologies of visible-light-driven BiVO4 photocatalysts. *Journal of nanoscience and nanotechnology, 14*(6), 4475-4480.

Xu, Y.-H., Liu, C.-J., Chen, M.-J., & Liu, Y.-Q. (2011). A review in visible-light-driven BiVO 4 photocatalysts. *International Journal of Nanoparticles, 4*(2-3), 268-283.

Yabuta, M., Takeda, A., Sugimoto, T., Watanabe, K., Kudo, A., & Matsumoto, Y. (2017). Particle Size Dependence of Carrier Dynamics and Reactivity of Photocatalyst BiVO4 Probed with Single-Particle Transient Absorption Microscopy. *The Journal of Physical Chemistry C, 121*(40), 22060-22066.

Yamasita, D., Takata, T., Hara, M., Kondo, J. N., & Domen, K. (2004). Recent progress of visible-light-driven heterogeneous photocatalysts for overall water splitting. *Solid State Ionics, 172*(1-4), 591-595.

Yan, Y., Sun, S., Song, Y., Yan, X., Guan, W., Liu, X., & Shi, W. (2013). Microwave-assisted in situ synthesis of reduced graphene oxide-BiVO4 composite photocatalysts and their enhanced photocatalytic performance for the degradation of ciprofloxacin. *Journal of hazardous materials, 250*, 106-114.

Yang, C.-T., Lee, W. W., Lin, H.-P., Dai, Y.-M., Chi, H.-T., & Chen, C.-C. (2016). A novel heterojunction photocatalyst, Bi 2 SiO 5/gC 3 N 4: Synthesis, characterization, photocatalytic activity, and mechanism. *RSC Advances, 6*(47), 40664-40675.

Yang, G., Li, S., Wu, M., & Wang, C. (2016). Zinc pyrovanadate nanosheets of atomic thickness: excellent Li-storage properties and investigation of their electrochemical mechanism. *Journal of Materials Chemistry A, 4*(28), 10974-10985.

Yang, L.-L., Zhao, Q., Willander, M., Yang, J., & Ivanov, I. (2009). Annealing effects on optical properties of low temperature grown ZnO nanorod arrays. *Journal of Applied Physics, 105*(5), 053503.

Yang, T., Xia, D., Chen, G., & Chen, Y. (2009). Influence of the surfactant and temperature on the morphology and physico-chemical properties of hydrothermally synthesized composite oxide BiVO4. *Materials Chemistry and Physics, 114*(1), 69-72.

Yang, W., Tan, G., Huang, J., Ren, H., Xia, A., & Zhao, C. (2015). Enhanced magnetic property and photocatalytic activity of UV-light responsive N-doped Fe2O3/FeVO4 heterojunction. *Ceramics International, 41*(1), 1495-1503.

Yao, W., Iwai, H., & Ye, J. (2008). Effects of molybdenum substitution on the photocatalytic behavior of BiVO 4. *Dalton Transactions*(11), 1426-1430.

Yin, W., Wang, W., Shang, M., Zhang, L., & Ren, J. (2009). Preparation of monoclinic scheelite BiVO4 photocatalyst by an ultrasound-assisted solvent substitution method. *Chemistry letters, 38*(5), 422-423.

Yu, Y., Niu, C., Han, C., Zhao, K., Meng, J., Xu, X., . . . Mai, L. (2016). Zinc pyrovanadate nanoplates embedded in graphene networks with enhanced electrochemical performance. *Industrial & Engineering Chemistry Research, 55*(11), 2992-2999.

Yu, Z., Lv, S., Ren, R., Cai, G., & Tang, D. (2017). Photoelectrochemical sensing of hydrogen peroxide at zero working potential using a fluorine-doped tin oxide electrode modified with BiVO 4 microrods. *Microchimica Acta, 184*(3), 799-806.

Zeki Bas, S., Cummins, C., Borah, D., Ozmen, M., & Morris, M. A. (2017). Electrochemical Sensing of Hydrogen Peroxide Using Block Copolymer Templated Iron Oxide Nanopatterns. *Analytical chemistry*.

Zeng, D., Xu, W., Ong, W.-J., Xu, J., Ren, H., Chen, Y., . . . Peng, D.-L. (2018). Toward noble-metal-free visible-light-driven photocatalytic hydrogen evolution: monodisperse sub–15 nm Ni2P nanoparticles anchored on porous g-C3N4 nanosheets to engineer 0D-2D heterojunction interfaces. *Applied Catalysis B: Environmental, 221*, 47-55.

Zhan, J.-H., Yang, X.-G., Wang, D.-W., Li, S., Xie, Y., Xia, Y., & Qian, Y. (2000). Polymer‐Controlled Growth of CdS Nanowires. *Advanced Materials, 12*(18), 1348-1351.

Zhang, A., & Zhang, J. (2009). Characterization of visible-light-driven BiVO4 photocatalysts synthesized via a surfactant-assisted hydrothermal method. *Spectrochimica Acta Part A: Molecular and Biomolecular Spectroscopy, 73*(2), 336-341.

Zhang, A., & Zhang, J. (2010a). Characterization and photocatalytic properties of Au/BiVO4 composites. *Journal of alloys and compounds, 491*(1-2), 631-635.

Zhang, A., & Zhang, J. (2010b). Effects of europium doping on the photocatalytic behavior of BiVO4. *Journal of hazardous materials, 173*(1-3), 265-272.

Zhang, J., Liu, W., Li, X., Zhan, B., Cui, Q., & Zou, G. (2009). Well-crystallized nitrogen-rich graphitic carbon nitride nanocrystallites prepared via solvothermal route at low temperature. *Materials Research Bulletin, 44*(2), 294-297.

Zhang, L., & Bahnemann, D. (2013). Synthesis of nanovoid Bi2WO6 2D ordered arrays as photoanodes for photoelectrochemical water splitting. *ChemSusChem, 6*(2), 283-290.

Zhang, L., Chen, D., & Jiao, X. (2006). Monoclinic structured BiVO4 nanosheets: hydrothermal preparation, formation mechanism, and coloristic and photocatalytic properties. *The Journal of Physical Chemistry B, 110*(6), 2668-2673.

Zhang, L., Ghimire, P., Phuriragpitikhon, J., Jiang, B., Gonçalves, A. A., & Jaroniec, M. (2018). Facile formation of metallic bismuth/bismuth oxide heterojunction on porous carbon with enhanced photocatalytic activity. *Journal of colloid and interface science, 513*, 82-91.

Zhang, Q., Gong, W., Wang, J., Ning, X., Wang, Z., Zhao, X., . . . Zhang, Z. (2011). Size-dependent magnetic, photoabsorbing, and photocatalytic properties of single-crystalline Bi2Fe4O9 semiconductor nanocrystals. *The Journal of Physical Chemistry C, 115*(51), 25241-25246.

Zhang, X., Ai, Z., Jia, F., Zhang, L., Fan, X., & Zou, Z. (2007). Selective synthesis and visible-light photocatalytic activities of BiVO4 with different crystalline phases. *Materials Chemistry and Physics, 103*(1), 162-167.

Zhang, Y., Yu, J., Kudo, A., & Zhao, X. (2008). Preparation of BiVO_4-MCM-41 Composite Catalyst and Its Photocatalytic Activity for Degradation of Methylene Blue [J]. *Chinese Journal of Catalysis, 7*, 008.

Zhang, Z., Wang, W., Shang, M., & Yin, W. (2010). Low-temperature combustion synthesis of Bi2WO6 nanoparticles as a visible-light-driven photocatalyst. *Journal of hazardous materials, 177*(1-3), 1013-1018.

Zhao, X., Lv, L., Pan, B., Zhang, W., Zhang, S., & Zhang, Q. (2011). Polymer-supported nanocomposites for environmental application: a review. *Chemical engineering journal, 170*(2-3), 381-394.

Zhou, Y., Vuille, K., Heel, A., Probst, B., Kontic, R., & Patzke, G. R. (2010). An inorganic hydrothermal route to photocatalytically active bismuth vanadate. *Applied Catalysis A: General, 375*(1), 140-148.

Zhu, J., Wei, S., Chen, M., Gu, H., Rapole, S. B., Pallavkar, S., . . . Guo, Z. (2013). Magnetic nanocomposites for environmental remediation. *Advanced Powder Technology, 24*(2), 459-467.

www.ingramcontent.com/pod-product-compliance
Lightning Source LLC
LaVergne TN
LVHW021047100526
838202LV00079B/4768